You're ok,
your
cat's ok

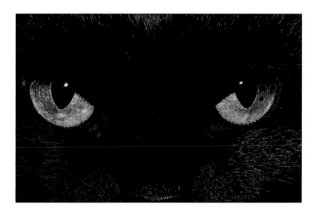

You're ok, your cat's ok

MARCUS SCHNECK
AND
JILL CARAVAN

CHARTWELL
BOOKS, INC.

A QUINTET BOOK

Published by Chartwell Books
A Division of Book Sales, Inc.
110 Enterprise Avenue
Secaucus, New Jersey 07094

This edition produced for sale
in the U.S.A., its territories
and dependencies only.

ISBN 1-55521-816-4

This book was designed and produced by
Quintet Publishing Limited
6 Blundell Street
London N7 9BH

Creative Director: Richard Dewing
Designer: Ian Hunt
Project Editor: Damian Thompson
Editor: Diana Vowles
Picture Researchers: Marcus Schneck and
Jill Caravan

Typeset in Great Britain by
Central Southern Typesetters, Eastbourne
Manufactured in Singapore by
Eray Scan Pte. Ltd.
Printed in Singapore by
Star Standard Industries Private Ltd.

DEDICATION:

To Tabby, Lucy, Benson, Jason, Bernie,
Pup, Fluffy, Muffy and Tiger, some of the
cats we have known and loved.

Contents

Introduction

Contemporary authors seem to be smitten by the idea of cats choosing their owners rather than vice versa. In our experience, it's been quite difficult for several years now to find a book on cats that does not offer the tale of some stray showing up on the doorstep, moving in and taking over the home of this author or that.

We won't claim that this doesn't happen, for we have heard of it happening from independent sources. We won't ever question whether it's actually happened to those dozens of authors. But, as an aside, we can't help but wonder: if cats do this at the rate suggested here, why are there any stray cats left in the world today?

Our real concern, however, with many of these enchanting tales is an underlying theme that they seem to share: that cats are something more than mere animals, something more like "little humans". And, because of this, they are deemed to have special mental powers, sometimes even mystical powers.

We love our cats. We've lived with cats since we were small children. We've enjoyed the companionship of these cats and many others that lived with friends and acquaintances – but we've never seen any evidence that they are anything other than members of the animal kingdom. Like all animals, they have their own special charms, intelligence, abilities and quirks. Every bit of evidence we've ever seen presented in support of what we call the "little human" syndrome – applying human qualities to the cat – can be completely explained by those animal qualities that are part of a cat's natural characteristics.

RIGHT *Unlike the rest of our domestic animals, cats made the decision to move in with us. This is part of the reason that we have a different relationship with them today than with our dogs.*

LEFT *Allow your cat some freedom to be a real cat and you'll be rewarded many times over with special insights into his world. He'll follow his natural instincts and you'll learn a great deal about what it means to be a cat, any species of cat.*

OPPOSITE ABOVE *Cats have cat emotions, cat thoughts and cat behaviours. Living with humans causes some alterations in all of these, but the perspective remains very much that of a cat.*

OPPOSITE BELOW *This ancient Egyptian bronze figurine wearing gold earrings was dedicated to the cult of Bast, goddess of fertility and love. The ancient Egyptians were the first to tame the cat.*

This is the general approach to much of the widely available information about cats that you're going to find throughout this book. We tend to question a great deal of what is passed off as fact. Our observations with our own cats and the observations of other cat owners we've known often gives us pause when compared to the current trends of expert opinion.

CAT FINDS MAN

For example, let's return to the idea that cats select their owners. There is some truth in it. They are our most independently minded companion animals, and they do make decisions like this. Unlike dogs, horses and the many other species that were brought into domestication by early man for his own reasons, cats decided that it was to their benefit to form the affiliation.

It appears that ancestors of today's domestic cat – more than likely some individuals of the African wild cat species that still exists today – moved into the granaries of ancient Egyptians. The cats' reason was simple: the granaries were overrun with rats, mice and other vermin. They presented hunting grounds packed with an unending supply of prey.

With the move came daily contact between cat and man, and gradual loss of wariness towards one another. Soon these smaller cats were replacing the large and more uncontrollable lions and cheetahs that had previously been worshipped in the temples. Then, as the cats multiplied and became more common, they started to show up as members of the household. At first only the wealthy families could afford the additional expense of maintaining an animal that still com-

If this book does nothing more than get you to think about the real reasons that motivate your cat, we've accomplished our primary goal. Such understanding doesn't make the cat any less fascinating or worthwhile as a companion, and it does make the relationship more enjoyable for both cat and man. Above all else, it provides the explanation for the majority of cat behaviour.

manded a certain amount of respect. But the feline supply continued to swell and soon most households had their own cat, which by that point had lost much of the respect it held previously.

RESPECTING THE RELATIONSHIP

As you can see, the cat's decision was based totally on natural animal needs. Acknowledging that doesn't cheapen the relationship that has since developed between cat and man – you shouldn't treat the cat with any less respect, affection or sensitivity. You can offer those and still allow the cat to retain its catness, those qualities that make the cat a cat. You won't expect human responses and emotions from your cat, and you can avoid the over-indulgence and the excessive pampering that has robbed so many cats of their natural dignity. Above all, you will be able to understand so much more of cats' behaviour than you ever could by adhering to the "little humans" approach. Owners should, in general, be far more ready to acknowledge and celebrate the differences between the human and feline worlds.

Inside that fur-covered head is a cat brain, the latest edition of thousands of years of cat ancestry. The behavioural pattern and instincts that have helped the species to survive are stored there, and the information is much closer to that in the lion's or tiger's brain than most of us would imagine.

No matter how we try to override that collected knowledge, nearly every movement, every thought and every reaction of our cats is governed by it to one extent or another. Certainly the experience of living with humans over many generations is part of that knowledge, but it is tempered by a cat's perspective.

As our title states, "You're OK, Your Cat's OK", and you'll both stay that way if you remember that you are a human and your cat is a cat. What follows is a guidebook to sharing your lives with that understanding.

CHAPTER ONE

The cat family and the cat lifestyle

erhaps it will be easier for you to accept your cat as an animal – albeit an animal that you love dearly and share your life with – if we first look at the history of the species.

The earliest known cat-like creatures emerged about 40 million years ago, about the same time as the earliest known dog-like creatures. At about this time in prehistory, the aeluroids (cat ancestors) and the arctoids (dog ancestors) went their separate ways from a common group of ancestors, known as miacids. The miacids, a group of small, arboreal carnivores, had been around for approximately 20 million years before that time.

In the above paragraph, you can find a very important point that will clarify a great deal about your cat. The ancestral line of our domestic cats,

LEFT *Cats are carnivores and predators. This doesn't make them "bad". It simply means that they have certain instincts and need certain things in their diet.*

OPPOSITE *The urge to hunt is instinctive, but the skills of the hunt and the kill are mostly learned. In today's world, many cats grow up never having received the full complement of those skills from their mothers.*

The Ancestors of the Cat

Dinictis Existed until 40 million years ago. About the size of a lynx. Long upper canines used to stab prey.

Pseudaelurus These animals more closely resembled today's cats, with long limbs and five-toed feet. They began to die out 25 million years ago.

which some well-meaning people today are trying to convert to the kinder and gentler vegetarian lifestyle, traces directly from the very first modern carnivores. The cat who is now sleeping on the sofa next to you has been genetically pro-grammed to eat meat for approximately 60 million years.

There are two ways for any creature to make its living as a meat-eater: hunt down prey and kill it, as carnivores generally do, or pick over the

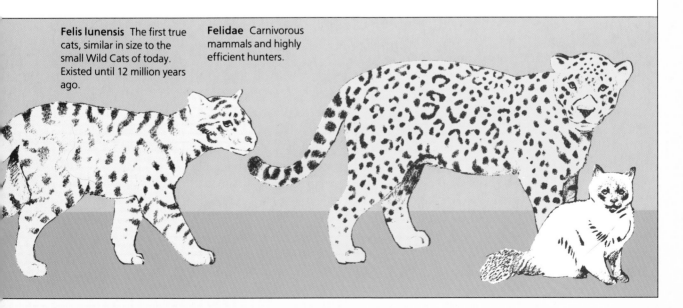

Felis lunensis The first true cats, similar in size to the small Wild Cats of today. Existed until 12 million years ago.

Felidae Carnivorous mammals and highly efficient hunters.

remains of something that died of natural causes or was killed by some other creature, as scavengers do. Although they were never above scavenging when the opportunity presented itself, the ancestors of our cats generally followed the path of the hunter.

From their common aeluroid genus, cats gradually evolved into today's three genera: *Acinonyx*, the cheetah; *Panthera*, the great cats, such as lions and tigers; and *Felis*, the small cats, including our domestic cat and several small wild cats such as the ocelot and serval.

Along the evolutionary way, many experiments were tried but failed. For example, the sabre-toothed cat *Smilodon* was a top predator until about 13,000 years ago, when it ceased to exist. It was an evolutionary failure, probably because of the extinction of its prey species. Whatever the reason, none of the modern cats

trace their lineage back to fearsome *Smilodon*.

So not only are our domestic cats the latest in a long line of hunters, they are the latest in a long line of hunters that were successful enough at hunting to survive and continue forward.

CANINES AND FELINES – DIFFERENT HUNTERS

Modern-day canines such as domestic dogs, wolves, dingoes, foxes and the like have also found their way along the evolutionary path as hunters, although supplementing the meat they could kill with a much wider array of vegetable matter than any cat ever considered.

However, canines and felines found different ways to pursue the hunting life, and this is crucial to our understanding of our domestic dogs and cats today. The canines developed as group

hunters, forming packs to work together in chasing down and killing their prey. The felines generally moved in the direction of the solitary hunter, relying on ambush and speed to take their prey.

There are, of course, exceptions to these rules. Some canines, such as the coyote of the western United States, more often hunt by themselves. (It's probably more than a coincidence that coyotes are excellent mousers and rely on rodents as a major portion of their diets.) Some felines, notably the lion, have chosen to live the group existence. (It's also interesting to note that the large, hoofed animals that the lions prey upon are rather similar to the principal prey species of canines such as the wolf.)

These hunting, and consequently lifestyle, "choices" made by long-gone ancestors are responsible for a large proportion of feline and canine behaviour today.

The pack lifestyle of the canine demands a highly socialized animal that acknowledges its subordinate standing to some members of its pack as well as its dominant standing over others.

It relies on and supports all the other members of its pack. Group activities are the cornerstones of existence, as is a strong rule of order.

The lone-hunter lifestyle of the feline requires an independent animal that generally enforces its dominance over weaker animals and avoids stronger ones. Survival as a lone hunter is almost wholly dependent upon the abilities, skills and knowledge of the individual. Independent action and circumstance-based decisions are the cornerstones of existence.

Of course, man's interference in this natural progression – better known as domestication – has changed the situation somewhat. With the ample food and shelter that we provide for our cats, group interaction is more likely. This has occurred naturally in communities of feral cats that have gathered across the globe wherever man's garbage is collected or disposed of. It helps to explain the group behaviour that we often find in homes that have more than one cat, or even sometimes a cat and a dog. With all their needs fulfilled, the cat's instinctive behaviour patterns are more pliable.

CHAPTER TWO

How does my cat love me?

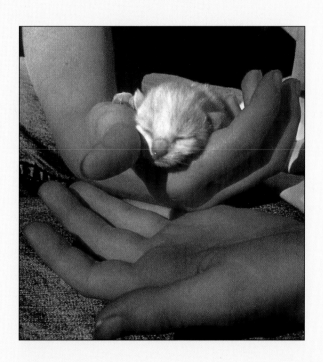

hy shouldn't our cats "love" us? In return for them being there, for doing pretty much what they want to do anyway and for putting up with an occasional show of affection from us, we give them everything they need for life: food, water, shelter and protection. We even throw in some sense-heightening activity from time to time, such as dangling a bit of string for them to bat at or rolling a ball of yarn for the chase.

Love may be too human a word for it, but in the normal human-cat relationship there is a

LEFT *Deep attachments can form between cat and human, with each one bringing his or her own species' emotions and ways of showing them into the relationship.*

bond. It's not the same as the human-dog bond, which arises from the dog's pack instincts, nor is it the same as the human-horse bond, which arises from the human's mastery over the horse.

Cats are not pack animals. About the only time they can genuinely be described as naturally social animals is during their kittenhood. Yes, they do get together for courtship and mating (but add a third cat to that picture and you have anything but social behaviour!). And, yes, cats kept together as housemates will often display group activity. But that stems more from our treatment of them as lifelong kittens rather than from a real longing for life in a group.

All of this, however, does not negate the fact that a bond generally does exist between humans and their cats, or cats and their humans depending upon your perspective on the situation. In many ways we take the place of a parent figure, providing nearly all of the basic needs for our cats. This naturally leads to a certain amount of dependency on the part of the cat, although not nearly as much mental and emotional dependency as a dog would feel. At the same time, it leads us into a certain dependence on the cat for some of our well-being as well.

Feline Affection

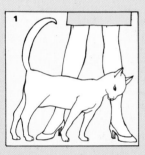

How do you politely introduce yourself? People shake hands, some dogs offer a paw. The really well-educated feline gently slides along human legs (1), maybe adding a gentle, purring vocal reminder of its arrival. Just in case you need a further message, a flaglike tail is raised in greeting. The message is clear and unmistakable – the cat wants to be introduced.

It takes a stern human to resist the attempts of the rubbing and licking cat to get itself picked up and petted (2). Another ploy is to lie on its back and look helpless. Once it has achieved its aim, the cat will continue to make contact. Sniffing a human's mouth or nose is a means of recognition and of saying "hello".

Man is always likely to take the poetry and romance out of anything. Some scientists insist that the reason cats lick human hands is to restore their deprived bodies with salt (3). Cat-lovers and less physiologically-minded students of behaviour believe that licking the hand is a mere preliminary to the much more obvious bond behaviours of mouth-to-mouth contact.

The lap is the cat's ultimate target (4). Some oriental types will not even give the human the option, but will simply leap on to a lap and settle down. The reason cats like lying on human laps is that they are comfortable and secure, and there can be few better reasons for doing anything.

All cat-lovers have been on the receiving end of a gentle, but persistent pounding by paws (5). This is sometimes assisted, most uncomfortably, by claws, and always with the full strength of the cat's forelegs. This is the normal behaviour of the nursing kitten and it lingers on. Kittens deprived of that sort of behaviour in their early lives are much more likely to inflict it on their owners.

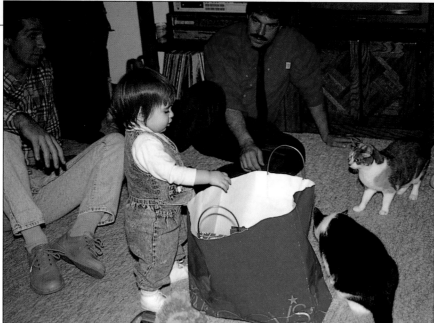

LEFT *Cats easily assimilate into the life of the household, to the extent that they allow themselves to join in. Some are more inclined to this than others.*

This is not a negative thing, unless that dependence becomes too strong for either party. A cat who spends nearly all of his time on his human's lap is probably too dependent – as is the human who forgoes activity outside the home to spend more time with his or her cat.

Let's insert one qualifier at this point. Cats are a popular companion for many homebound senior citizens. The links between these people and their cats are naturally going to be somewhat stronger and more intense than in many other human-cat relationships.

LEFT *Only a cat that is very comfortable in its relationship with a human would allow itself to be this exposed, even while asleep or almost asleep. Such chance-taking is the ultimate show of acceptance in the feline mind.*

OPPOSITE *Some cats are more accepting than others of the rough-handling that comes with the affections of children. In a wild situation such contact would almost always be taken as threat or attack, but life with humans has made an impact on the mental attitudes of our cats.*

CATS AND CHILDREN

At the other end of the age spectrum, cats can also develop warm relationships with children. Although dogs are the consummate baby-lovers, cats too can be wonderful around kids, from newborns to teenagers. With the exception of the occasional anti-social animal, a cat's attitude towards young humans is mostly determined by the initial human actions towards the cat.

When a newborn baby is brought into the home, the typical reaction by the parents and grandparents is to exclude the cat. How would you feel if you had suddenly been moved from one of the focal points in the home to a sideline position? All your attempts to garner attention that were previously seen as cute are now spurned and even discouraged. Is it any wonder that the cat soon comes to greet the new addition with a certain amount of resentment?

The solution is obvious. Include the cat in as much as possible that concerns the baby. Under close supervision, allow the cat to sniff the baby. When you're involved with the baby and the cat

is nearby, be certain to mention the cat's name occasionally, offer it some praise and have some physical contact. Make sure that you're not cutting back too severely on playtime with the cat because of time spent with the baby.

The cat's relationship with children is to a large part determined by the approach that the humans adopt. Let's face the fact that children are noisy, rough and erratic. They get on our nerves, so why not our cats' nerves as well?

Pulling her tail, grabbing her ears, running at her, carrying her about like a doll are all guaranteed to put the cat off from further contact and so must be prevented. Children must also be taught that the cat is completely off-limits at certain times, primarily when she is eating, using the litter box or sleeping.

Many cat owners seem to assume that cats and children mix even less than oil and water. After a few negative experiences, they give up trying to introduce the cat to children on the basis that it seems best for everyone concerned simply to keep them apart. With just a bit of attention to

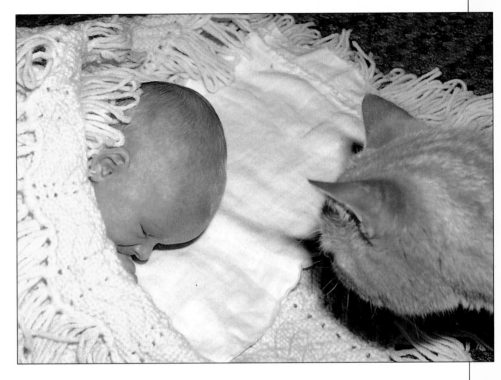

RIGHT *Cats are naturally curious about any addition to the home, especially a new baby. As long as adult supervision is constant, the cat poses no danger to the infant.*

BELOW *Quiet, peaceful activities are more likely to attract the interest and participation of cats, although their attention spans can be pretty short. Natural circumstances normally involve a wild cat in any given activity for relatively brief periods.*

the first couple of encounters, however, felines and young humans can learn to enjoy each other's company.

The relationship of your cat with children should begin before the first physical contact is made. Because children are slightly easier to train – only by a whisker – direct your instructions to the child.

He should wait for the cat to approach him, which really won't take that long given the curious nature of most cats. When the approach does come, he should not reach out to grab or pet the cat. Instead he should slowly and smoothly hold out his hand towards the cat's nose, for some getting-to-know-you sniffing. If that seems to bring an overall friendly reaction from the cat, the child can pet her gently and talk to her softly. Having the child use the cat's name, or other "cuddle" words that the cat seems to appreciate at other times, will increase the chances of the encounter being a promising one.

Regardless of how well a cat–child session may seem to be proceeding, babies and young children

LEFT *When the cat wants attention it makes little difference what you're involved in or what deadlines you face. The cat functions on its own level, fulfilling its most basic needs.*

OPPOSITE *Left to develop naturally, as much as is realistically possible, the cat-child relationship can develop into a wonderful and special thing.*

The Affectionate Cat

Cats demonstrate their affection in several ways, most of which relate to their natural and instinctive display of emotions. Rubbing up against us is the most common and widely recognized of these.

Another is licking our hands. Many people write this activity off as a simple search for the salt in our sweat, but cats lick one another in the same way as part of their grooming. It's definitely a bonding mechanism.

When your cat sucks on your hand or arm, or kneads you with his forefeet, accept this as the ultimate show of trust, affection and dependency. The cat often does this after a particularly soothing session of petting and stroking. He is acting like he did during his kittenhood, when he kneaded his mother's underside to prompt her teats to produce milk. The cat is momentarily regressing into those wonderfully comfortable and secure days, and redirecting his fond memories on to you. In short, the cat is proclaiming you to be his current mother figure.

The more you respond to such shows of affection, the tighter will become the bond between you and your cat. Lavish your love on the animal. Feel free to let him know the full extent of your affection.

should *never* be left alone with a cat. No matter how much you trust the cat, or the child, there is always the possibility of one of them overreacting to something the other does and attempting to inflict pain on the other. What started out as a happy relationship can turn into an ugly one when you have to decide who did what to whom and whether the cat is stable enough to stay in the family (it's never a question of whether or not to get rid of the kid). The cats are usually the losers in these cases, which is unfortunate because the real blame should be placed on the parents who failed to follow this most basic rule of cat-child relationships.

Cats that have been introduced to children in a casual, non-confrontational manner are generally very open to meetings with other children. If the child can be contained within the cat's acceptable parameters for human behaviour towards her, the relationship can proceed much like any cat-human bond, complete with heartfelt affection.

BONDING WITH YOUR CAT

Many of us mistakenly treat our pets as children. Because of their drive for comfort and security in their lives, they will be happy to accommodate us as far as it serves their needs. However, to expect a cat to give as much as it gets is a certain route to disappointment, as it also is to believe subconsciously that the cat will always be there for you, even though you know she probably cannot live more than 10 to 15 years.

You should give as much as you can to the relationship and allow your cat the freedom to do the same. Even human-to-human relationships where a tally is kept of all that is given and taken by each party are headed for problems. Expecting equality of give and take will not lead to the sort of bonding that will give you and your cat the most enjoyable relationship.

In animal terms, bonding is the pairing of two creatures who develop a long-term connection as the result of shared experiences and dependency.

Bonding is not only satisfying, it is also essential in maintaining a well-mannered cat as part of your life and home.

The process begins from your very first contact with the cat, whether that occurs when she is just a kitten or when she is well into maturity. Usually you have no idea of what the cat experienced before she came into your life. She may have socialized with other cats and humans, she may have had no contact with others or she may have suffered plenty of negative contact.

You must first communicate to her that she is safe with and accepted by you. Long before you begin to think about showing her around the house or beginning her training, you must establish the maximum comfort and security level possible. Only then will she be receptive.

When you first bring the cat into your home, don't overwhelm her by allowing the family to crowd around and try to touch her. It's best to introduce her to this new environment on a one-to-one basis. Gently allow her to look around

OPPOSITE *By providing ample quantities of all the basics of a cat's life we have made room for a much more social existence than wild felines normally enjoy. We've eliminated most of the environmental reasons for competition.*

RIGHT *Babies and children often want to reach out and touch animals, which can disturb some cats but is accepted warmly by others. Individual temperaments, coloured by a sense of security, determine the actual outcome of such an encounter.*

CAT WATCHING TIP

Compare sleeping positions with this chart that correlates position with electroencephalogram (EEG) readings.

Your cat is most alert when awake (1), but its brain waves slow down and get larger as it falls into light sleep, maybe sitting or partially lying down (2). Getting really comfortable and falling into a deep sleep (3) results in a physically very relaxed cat, but one whose brain waves are similar to those when the cat is awake. Positions alternate as the cat drifts in and out of light and deep sleep (4), before it awakens and returns to its alert and upright position and its normal waking brain waves (5).

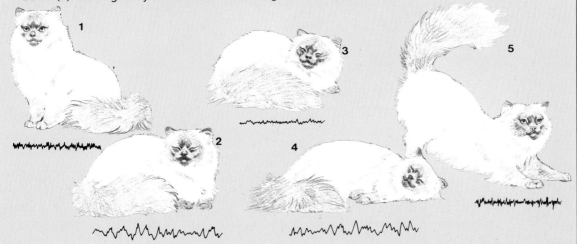

and examine whatever she will at first. When she seems somewhat familiarized, bring in members of the family individually and let them gently touch her and get to know her, and her them. Other pets, which should have been kept in another room until now, should be introduced last, although not after too long a wait.

She won't have any understanding of your words at this point, but she will be on constant watch for any clues that she can draw from your tone and touch. Gently and soothingly are how both should be delivered.

At first, and probably for a longer period than you're going to appreciate, you won't get much tenderness from your cat. She has an entirely new territory to establish. After all, who knows what dangers may lurk in it? Give her the "space" she needs to discover just how completely safe and secure you've made her.

She may not want much physical contact at all at first, but you can rely on her intelligence to keep her posted on just who it is that seems to be fulfilling her every need. Eventually, if she hasn't been pressed too hard on the issue, she will probably initiate contact on her own. That's your cue to really lay on the love and affection in as large a quantity as you can manage while still maintaining that atmosphere of calmness and gentleness.

Of course, if the cat has not taken it on herself to do this within a week or so of being brought into the home, you may need to coax it out of her. Approach slowly, as near to her level as you can – sitting, if that's the best you can do; kneeling is better yet; hands and knees is still better; and on your belly is best of all. Speak gently and soothingly. Some morsels of food would definitely not hurt.

Once the bonding has begun and has then continued on a regular basis, it might become a ritual that the cat now expects as part of its everyday life. (See "The importance of ritual" on p. 53.)

LEFT *Any spot that provides the comfort and security that they constantly crave will be attractive to our cats. For a deeper relationship try to become part of that comfort and security by observing what it is that gives these qualities to your cat and how you can enhance them.*

CHAPTER THREE

Communication
is a two-way process

Obviously Broomhilda was trying to tell us something. There was a certain, growing impatience in her meowing, a genuine urgency in her tone, an anxious stiffness in her posture. But she might just as well have been handing us a copy of *Pravda*, with the Russian words circled to spell out her message. It just wasn't getting through to us.

Normally at this point in the evening she would be curled up in her kitty-hutch in the kitchen rather than working, with only sporadic success, to distract our attention from the sitcom we were watching.

Finally, at a commercial break, I gave into her efforts. Broomhilda was happy to lead me into the kitchen. At first nothing out of the ordinary presented itself. Everything seemed to be in place. The water bowl was full. The litter box was clean . . . well, clean enough. Her bed was in place, looking as comfortable as usual.

I was muttering something quite unflattering about "that crazy cat" and turning to head back into the living room when I noticed that one of the windows had slipped open a bit. A steady stream of cool autumn air was flowing into the kitchen. It was just enough to lower the room temperature by a few degrees, and Broomhilda had always been a rather sensitive creature.

Shortly after the window had been closed – probably enough time for the kitchen to return to room temperature – Broomhilda was gone from the living room. Sure enough, she was sound asleep in her kitty-hutch, just as she usually was at this time of the evening.

OK, so it's not an inspirational, thought-provoking tale of a cat bringing help through dozens of miles of wilderness to save the life of her injured, near-death owner. None of our cats has ever seemed to have some life-and-death messages to impart. Instead of that noble movie

OPPOSITE AND RIGHT *The natural cat-to-cat greeting consists of sniffing and licking one another's face. Your cat will seek this same greeting contact with you, unless he's been rebuked too often. Accommodate his urge for this and you'll greatly strengthen the bond that the two of you are constantly building.*

image of pet communication, our cats have usually wanted to tell us about some problem in their lives, something that was interfering with their normal everyday comfort.

The point is this: while Broomhilda didn't have the language to tell us specifically what she thought needed our attention, she had learned a method of getting the basic message across, at least enough to spur some action on our part. She was using the communication devices at her disposal: voice and body language. In both of these areas, cats are amply supplied.

VOICE

The purr is both the most universally recognized and the most widely misunderstood trait of the domestic cat. Even the basic mechanism that produces the sound is still under debate today, thousands of years after cat and man first linked up. Theories about this mechanism include: motion in the cat's blood as it passes through the chest area, with the resulting sound being amplified by the diaphragm; inhaled air causing the false vocal cords, known as vestibular folds, to run against one another; or contraction of the larynx muscles.

Regardless of how a purr is produced, there can be no doubt that the sound is intricately linked to the cat's emotions. With that said and agreed upon, we once again enter into the area of debate. Purring has been translated as meaning everything from supreme happiness to drowsiness to comfort to anxiety to pain, as well as every emotion in between.

ABOVE AND RIGHT
Grooming one another is a comfortable, social activity among cats which harks back to their days as kittens. It is an activity that they will share with those humans with whom they've become very comfortable.

In our experience, the following purr-types indicate these emotions.

☐ Coarse and loud: Contented and comfortable.

☐ Swift and terse: Fear or intimidation.

☐ Soft and flowing: Drowsy, almost asleep.

☐ Fast and highly segmented: Expectation, anticipation.

However, like all explanations of what the purr really means, this is only drawn from observations of certain cats. It's a fine starting point for someone new to the cat fancy, as long as it's gradually tempered with direct observation of the individual cat in question. Just as there are humans who stutter, lisp and choose their words poorly, there are cats who have their own particular uses of the purr.

Cats also have several other vocalizations beyond the purr. When uttered urgently, the meow generally indicates that the cat is requesting, sometimes almost demanding, something that is due him. In a softer, almost questioning tone, the meow most often represents a gentle

The Purring Puzzle

The vocal apparatus of cats is very different from that of humans. Vocal sounds are produced by changes in the tension of muscles in the throat and mouth, and by changes in the speed of air moving over the vocal cords, which are stretched across the larynx. The vibration of the "false" vocal cords may be involved in purring, though the basic mechanism that produces the sound is still under debate today.

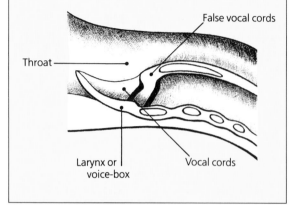

False vocal cords

Throat

Larynx or
voice-box

Vocal cords

inquiry into something. With considerably more volume, it can indicate anger.

The spitting sound seems to be reserved for a more intense anger, often when the cat has been startled. If the ears are held flat to the head and the face is virtually lacking in expression, the spit is a warning to back off. Many cats also employ a snorting growl as a warning, and a yowling scream as an even more direct threat. A teeth-chattering twitter reveals a high level of excitement, such as when the evening's meal is being emptied from can to bowl. The combination purr-murmur is the cat-to-cat greeting, sometimes shared with a human who has bonded very thoroughly with the cat.

And, of course, the shrieking wail that wakes us from the soundest of sleeps in the middle of the night is the territorial mating call of the male. Both sexes will emit a similar noise when experiencing pain.

LEFT *The cat on the left is exhibiting a defensively submissive posture in response to the aggressively dominant stance adopted by his opponent on the right.*

OPPOSITE *Most domestic cats have a wide range of vocalizations, each with its own special meaning that we humans may or may not understand. Given time, however, an observant owner can come to catalogue a great majority of his cat's calls.*

BODY LANGUAGE

Body language is just as important as vocalizations in cat communication – perhaps even more so. Again, you will need to temper all of our guidelines with direct observations of your cat.

A cat that holds his body erect and his head low, with the definite appearance of attack readiness, is a cat who is secure in his dominance over the current situation. If the cat felt subordinate, his body would be held low to the floor in a crouch that suggests a cringing defence. A more aggressively defensive attitude is displayed through an arched back that makes the cat appear much larger than he really is. This last display might also be a bluff to conceal fear.

When a cat throws himself on to his side on the floor or rolls on to his side with paws (but not claws) extended he is usually issuing an invitation for some play. This action generally comes when the cat is feeling drowsy or lazy. You've probably caught him asleep, just waking up or about to

snooze. If he had been more awake, he probably would have walked over to you and rubbed against your leg.

Although it is much more common in dogs, some cats will rear up on their hind legs as a greeting. The reason for this is the same as in dogs: we're so much bigger than cats that they cannot perform the traditional face-rubbing/smelling ritual. As a poor substitute, they are at least directing their greeting where it should be placed. This is the same instinctive reaction that sends a cat up on to a piece of furniture in greeting. You can continue your bonding with the cat in either of these instances by bending down to allow face-to-face contact.

Positioning himself in front of you while you are walking is a request for you to follow, probably to fulfil some need of the cat's. The tail is another mirror to his emotions. For example, in the "please follow me" posture the tail will generally be held upright. The upright position

OPPOSITE *An arched back with fur standing on end is the ultimate show of alarm or threat in the domestic cat. It shares these physical reactions with the various wild species of cat.*

RIGHT *Nearly every thought of the cat is telegraphed by his tail. Held vertically, but not fluffed out, as shown, the tail is signalling a generally friendly attitude.*

BELOW *Look into your cat's eyes and you can see his mind in action. The eyes often reflect the general health of the animal as well.*

at other times represents a friendly attitude or a state of pleasure and comfort. If that vertical tail is also puffed out like a feather the cat is experiencing fear. An arched variation on the vertical is the cat's signal for wanting to play a chase-and-catch type of game. When the cat sits at a window and watches birds or squirrels outside, or otherwise observes something with anticipation, the tail will twitch and sway slowly.

CAT WATCHING TIP

Has your cat ever curled its upper lip back as though it were attempting to dislodge a food particle from between its teeth? At the same time, you may have noticed that it was quite erect and alert. This is an action known as flehming. With it, the cat is drawing odours to an organ on the roof of its mouth, an additional "smelling" apparatus.

Facial Expressions

Perky ears and relaxed whiskers mark the face of a happy cat (1). An angered cat will push back its erect ears, narrow its pupils to slits, and push its whiskers forward (2). Flattened ears and whiskers and widened pupils show that a cat is frightened (3). A cat opens its pupils, perks up its ears, and bristles its whiskers forward when hunting and playing (4). A cat that is in ecstasy when being patted or when satisfied relaxes its eyes and whiskers (5).

LEFT *This cat is uncertain about both its control of the situation and the intentions of the child. Its reaction could vary from calming down to flight or defence.*

OPPOSITE *Go ahead, discuss anything and everything with your cat. It's healthy for both of you, as long as you know what to expect in return. The cat really only understands those words that you have conditioned it to understand as meaningful to its life.*

At the other end of the cat there is an equal repertoire of body language. Half-closed eyes signal a contented, comfortable animal, more than likely on the verge of a quick snooze. Wide-open eyes, combined with erect whiskers and ears, are usually displayed by a cat who feels in control of the current situation. If the eyes are tensely closed to narrow slits and the ears are twisted sideways, you are facing a cat that is less certain of his mastery of the situation and is probably considering (however subliminally) the options of attack or escape.

Occasionally a cat will be seen in what looks almost like a sneer or a grimace. The cat will suddenly stop in its tracks, open its mouth a little and draw back its upper lip. This action, known

as the flehmen response, really carries not special message for you, other than perhaps that there is some smell worthy of note in the air.

The flehmen response is most commonly associated with males testing females for readiness for mating. However, it is also applied to other particularly appealing scents. In the roof of the cat's mouth is something known as the Jacobsen's organ, which is extremely sensitive to the chemicals in the air that actually make up smells.

The mouth, or more precisely the tongue, can also give us signals about the cat's state of mind. When the cat is becoming irritated or perplexed by a situation, but nonetheless remains interested in it, his tongue flicks out and curves upward

Sixth Sense – or Sharper Senses?

Occasions are sometimes reported of an owner being alerted to some impending danger of some unexpected event by a cat. These instances are commonly attributed to that special sixth sense that cats are often said to possess.

There is no scientific evidence to support the idea of this sixth sense. It seems more likely these "premonitions" that cats sometimes seem to have are the result of the superior senses of the hunter, particularly the sense of hearing.

Cats hear a much greater range of sound than we do, from noises that are far too faint for our ears to pick up to ultrasonic sounds much higher in pitch than we can hear. Their upper range is even greater than that of the dog, which is better known for this ability (humans and dogs can hear sounds in slightly lower pitches than cats can). On top of this greater ability, the hunter inside our cats keeps them constantly alert for important sounds.

Cats are also much better able to locate the source of sounds. Testing has shown that some can differentiate one sound from another when the sources are 3 ft (90 cm) from the cat and only 3 in (7.5 cm) apart. Their brain accomplishes this by measuring the intensity and timing of the different sounds.

Cat eyesight isn't much stronger than our own, until the light goes down. While even cats can't see in absolute darkness, they do see very well in what to most of us humans seems to be total darkness. To accomplish this, the pupil, cornea and lens of the cat's eye are larger than ours and a special structure known as the tapetum lucidum is located behind the retina. The tapetum lucidum is made up of a dozen or more layers of highly reflective material. These arrangements allow the cat's eyes to gather much more light than ours can.

The cat's sense of smell is also greater than ours, but lesser than that of the dog. Length of nose is a rather effective indicator of this ability. The noses of some long-snouted pooches carry nearly 150 million nerve endings, while most feline noses have in the neighbourhood of 20 million and we humans struggle along with a scant 5 million.

ABOVE *During the Middle Ages, cats suffered terrible persecution at the hands of superstitious people who believed that witches could change themselves into cats and back again at will. So many cats were burned alive that the species was almost extinct in Europe in 1400. These witches are depicted accompanied by a cat, a dog, a mouse and an owl – their "familiars", or demons in the form of animals.*

over his nose swiftly and repeatedly. It's an outward reflection of the should-I-stay-or-should-I-go conflict that's taking place in the animal's mind.

Physical contact is another important means of communication for our felines. Claws and teeth communicate an obvious, if undesirable, emotion. Rubbing against your leg, on the other hand, displays the affection that the cat is feeling, not to mention marking you as a familiar friend with his scent glands.

LEFT *Cats gain much of their understanding about what we're saying through the tones we use in addressing them. Again, their reactions are based on the conditioning we've imparted to them through previous experiences.*

Because our cats are living in the unnatural world that we have created, they will also bring some of their man-made surroundings into the communication. For example, some have learned to ring a doorbell when they want to go out.

IS ANY OF WHAT I'M SAYING GETTING THROUGH?

Try this experiment with your cat. Look directly at her, maintain as much of a poker face as you can and, in a harsh, gruff voice, say "good cat" or whatever word you normally use to show your pleasure with the animal. Note her reaction. At least an hour later, look directly at the cat again, maintain that same poker face and, in a soft, gentle voice, say the same words. Compare this reaction with the one earlier.

Unless you normally give such conflicting signals to your cat and she has adjusted her reactions accordingly, you will notice that the way you said the words was much more important than what you said.

Of course, cats do learn many of our words, assigning to them meanings that they derive from their own instincts and experiences. Those cat-interpretations of our words are probably quite different from what the words actually mean to us humans. We really have no way of knowing whether the cat that answers to its name is coming because it somehow associates the name

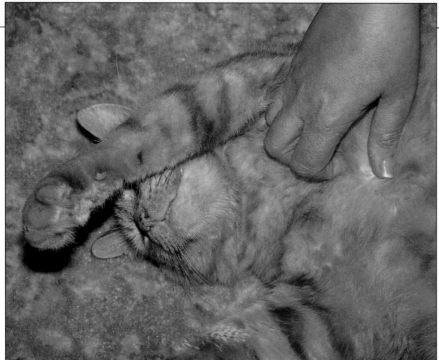

LEFT *Physical contact is an essential means of communication for our cats. This cat is having much more than a particular tickle-spot massaged.*

OPPOSITE *From their own perspective, our cats are aware of the love that we lavish on them. To the feline mind, what we intend as loving attention is translated into aspects of comfort and security.*

with itself or because it associates the sound with good things happening to it, such as being fed or stroked.

There is some evidence that shorter, more direct words are more readily remembered by cats. For this reason, a name like "Puff" will bear results much quicker and more consistently than something like "Mister Bennington", which is the actual name of one cat we've known. The same concept should be applied to commands that we want to teach to our cats.

We've often longed for some type of device that could translate the thoughts of our pets into words or symbols that we could understand. Think of the insight we could gain into these animals' minds! On the other hand, there might be much more "dead air" in those brain waves than we currently believe.

Until such a futuresque device is perfected, we shall have to rely on observation – and from observation we can tell that the tone of voice is one of the cat's chief clues as to what we mean.

Although our language is greatly evolved from the days when our cave-dwelling ancestors lived on an equal basis with the other animals,

CAT WATCHING TIP

The next time your cat raises its hackles in an apparently quiet house, check more closely for the noise you *didn't* hear. Because cats' senses are so much more attuned than humans', it's likely that your cat actually has felt, seen, smelled or heard something that interests it.

Have a check around. Your cat's whiskers may have felt a slight draught, maybe from a small crack in your walls that you've never noticed. Maybe it saw movement, something fast and minute. Maybe it smelled another cat or some other creature outside, somewhere on its territory. Or maybe its ears picked up a high-pitched noise from the animal kingdom.

we've retained much in our tones that is similar to the tones of animal vocalizations – and tone is the real means of communication in the animal world. Your tone will convey your anger, your fear, your friendliness or your agression to the cat no matter what words you choose.

Everything you say to your cat is considered in the context of situation and body language.

This explains how our cats, and our dogs for that matter, seem to sense when we're sick or in pain. They're not applying some mystical sixth sense. Our body language reveals great detail to

them. They respond, often by curling up with us in the bed, because they are genuinely concerned about the unusual "vibes" they are picking up on and also because they enjoy spending time on the bed while we are there.

However, cats also come to expect some understanding of what we mean from the words we say. The most highly socialized cats will even go out of their way to pick up the meanings of new words that you're not even intending to teach them. By listening and observing, they are able to piece together such bits of our language. You'll probably first notice this one day when you say something like "tuna fish" to another human and see your cat scurry from the room in the direction of the cupboard where the canned fish is stored.

Similarly, with a well-trained cat, you may eventually notice that she is reacting to words you've taught her even when you are not saying them directly to her or in the context in which you've tried to teach them.

We have been told for generations that cats cannot be trained like dogs, and many cats do their darndest to maintain that image. But look at it from a different perspective and you'll see that it's to the cat's advantage to pick up on some of our words simply to increase the comfort of her life. You can bet the cat has a sense of this.

The simple fact that she hears your voice in that special calm and soothing tone adds to her security. Contrary to the portrayal in countless movies and television sitcoms, talking to your cat is not a crazy thing to do. That is, unless you expect to hear human language as a response or to impart understanding of concepts far beyond the simple life-pursuits of a cat.

If you are clear that you won't be achieving either of these things, go ahead and talk to the cat – it's psychologically beneficial for both of you.

You'll feel a bit more relaxed after the "conversation", and your cat's comfort and security levels will be raised. Bonding will take place meanwhile.

The exact topic under discussion doesn't really matter, but the more you can work in those words that you are certain you cat knows, the more enjoyable she will find the session. If possible, get down to her level. Lie on the floor and look directly into her eyes. While direct eye contact between unfamiliar animals is often a pre-

ABOVE *Treating your cat to some special attention is fine. The cat will respond in kind. However, expecting human responses can lead to disappointment. The cat can respond only in cat terms and in related ways that it has been conditioned to use.*

cursor to aggression, in those beings that a cat is already familiar with the same gesture is entirely positive. Use a soft, comforting tone of voice and stroke her as you speak.

CHAPTER FOUR

How intelligent is my cat?

We've counted the number of words that we are certain beyond a doubt that our cocker spaniel Timber knows and reacts predictably to, and the number is somewhere in the neighbourhood of 85.

We've never done a similar count for any of the cats we've lived with. There never seemed to be any reason to do it. The concept of commands, or more exactly commands being given by a human who must be obeyed, is vague at best to the cat. This is not to say that some cats haven't been taught a healthy array of commands, but we've never seen the cat that can be counted on 100 per cent of the time to do what is expected when a certain command is given.

Some commands and non-command words will be conditioned into even the most untrained house cat's "vocabulary" through constant exposure to them and/or a system of rewards. But, with cats, obeying commands seems to rest at their whim. If the command fits in with the current wants and needs of the cat, it probably will be obeyed. Otherwise, it will probably not.

So obedience to commands is in no way a measure of intelligence in cats. As with every living animal species on the face of the earth, it is a safe assumption that there are smart cats and stupid cats.

THE THINKING CAT

Some of the smartest cats we've known have not been the most consistent in following our commands. When they did choose to obey, and as long as their attention span held out, they were

LEFT *Obedience to commands and the ability to perform tricks are reflections more of the cat's socialization into the household than of the animal's overall intelligence.*

OPPOSITE *Cats are highly intelligent animals, but that intelligence must be measured in cat terms rather than with our human definitions. In this measure, survival and level of comfort/security are the true gauges of intelligence.*

very expert and precise in their execution of the orders. However, as soon as they tired of the activity or something else caught their highly active attention, that was the end of the exercise.

Just as obedience to commands cannot be taken as the ultimate measure of a cat's intelligence, neither can any of the animal-IQ tests that have been developed. The same trigger- or colour-matching paraphernalia that can occupy a dog or a chimpanzee, for lengthy periods will just as likely put a cat to sleep.

However, although we can't accurately measure our cats' IQs, we know there is a feline intelligence within their brains. The signs of that intelligence are unmistakable. Cats are relatively cautious animals, often sizing up situations, evaluating alternatives and making choices based on risk-benefit equations. They have an almost unquenchable curiosity about their world, making regular explorations into both known and unknown areas. They are independent-minded creatures, as anyone who has spent long afternoons trying to teach a command can attest.

They are problem-solvers, quick to discover and perfect techniques to satisfy their basic needs. The getting of food is probably the area where most of us have encountered this ability. Cats

OPPOSITE *The attention span of many cats is rather short, while the desire for rest and sleep is very strong. This doesn't indicate lesser intelligence, just different needs from our own.*

LEFT *The exploratory nature of our cats is one indication that there is some fairly powerful intelligence at work in those little heads.*

learn quickly which end of a bottle the milk pours from and how to make that happen, or how to cause that special sound with the electric can opener that always signals mealtime.

Various studies have shown that cats raised with plenty of stimuli, such as handling, hunting and play, develop greater abilities in all the areas we've just discussed. The importance of any animal's adolescent period of exploration and learning in relation to its later successes in life is another measure of intelligence.

Hunting is the most well-known example of this process. While hunting is an instinct kittens are born with, the techniques of finding prey, stalking it, capturing it, killing it and eating it are learned abilities. They are passed on from one generation to the next by the queen to her kittens.

Cats deprived of this learning experience as kittens – perhaps because they and their mother were never allowed outdoors – generally do not

acquire the skills needed to become successful hunters. The instinct is still alive within them, as demonstrated by their tail-flicking interest in birds outside the window, but they usually don't have what it takes to follow through on that urge.

For those cats that have been given this ability, remembering productive hunting sites is one of the tasks to which they choose to employ their memory capacity. Watch your cat the next time you let her out to roam the garden. Certain spots will require her immediate attention. Similarly, the warmest, cosiest sunning windows and the actions needed to tell the human that food or play is wanted are all readily recalled.

There we have the crux of this whole question about cat intelligence. Catch them in the act of using their memory or their reasoning to their own ends and on their own terms and you'll be amazed. Try to direct those same powers into behaviour considered to be desirable by humans,

such as not ripping the new upholstery, and you'll be frustrated as often as not.

Yet another measure of intelligence comes in the form of the many tales we hear of cats finding their way home across significant distances. Rest assured that cats can remember the location of their homes, but don't assume that it is their owners and families that they are seeking. It's the territory that they've claimed and developed that draws them home.

Evidence suggests that cats perform this feat by combining two mechanisms: an internal biological clock that measures time in terms much more elemental than the 24 equal segments we've assigned rather arbitrarily to each day; and a sense for the angle of the sun's rays on the cat's home territory, learned over time.

This ability, also observed in other creatures such as migrating caribou and birds, is termed natural celestial navigation. In human terms – although we've lost much of our ability in this area – it's similar to knowing that you've come towards the sun in leaving your home for a hike and must return with the sun behind you to find your home once again.

Finally, we do have some hard data from science to point towards cat intelligence. This comes in the form of electroencephalogram (EEG) readings of cat brain waves during sleep. Evidence points to the fact that cats experience something similar to our dreams during periods of deep sleep, which is characterized by rapid eye movement and thus labelled REM sleep.

For those of us without thousands of dollars'-worth of such scientific measuring devices in our homes, our cats provide some external evidence of this as well. Watch your cat the next time you notice her in deep sleep, which seems to be about 30 per cent of the 16 to 18 hours most cats spend sleeping every day. You'll see the movement of the paws, the changing positions of the body, the tail flicking, and the ears and whiskers twitching. Most cats will also utter calls, meows, purrs and even shrieks during these dreams.

THE IMPORTANCE OF RITUAL

All animals, including our domestic cats, survive in part through the application of a standard set of rituals to their everyday lives. The rituals will vary from one animal to the next, but they all have some.

To the wild ancestors of our cats, the most important rituals involved mating, hunting down and killing prey, and maintaining the secrecy of the den location. Sub-rituals that were part of the primary rites included such activities as encountering competing cats and avoiding conflict or besting that competitor, and teaching the young to become successful at the business of being cats.

These rituals are still very much alive in the cats with whom we share our homes. You can see some of them in practice nearly every day.

Life in a man-made environment has resulted in new rituals being developed. The most obvious of these, at least with those cats that are fed on a regular schedule, can be observed at mealtime. There is no standard form here – the particular aspects vary from one cat to the next in their different situations. However, for every cat, you can be certain that there is a noticeable ritual associated with food.

OPPOSITE *Cats begin learning from a very early age. Their mothers are their primary teachers, and hunting skills are among the things they pass on to their kittens.*

RIGHT *While the things they choose to remember are sometimes less than impressive to us humans, such as the choice sunning spots around the home, cats nevertheless display good memories.*

Your arrival home each day is probably the source of another. Do you often find your cat in the same location when you open the front door in the evening? If you have a day off, but spend it mostly away from the cat in some other part of the house, will you find her in the same spot about the time you normally come through the door? What about if you come in through another entrance? Such questions will be similarly revealing about other major times of the day that involve the cat. If she is allowed to sleep on your bed, she probably has her just-before-bed rituals that must be observed.

A friend of ours got into the habit of ambushing her Maine Coon Cat, Tibsy, each evening as the cat came to investigate her absence when she took the dinner dishes from the dining room to the kitchen. She would hide on the far side of the doorway between the two rooms and jump out at Tibsy when he entered the kitchen.

OTT 48

LEFT *Some rituals are more eagerly awaited than others. Regular feeding times help to enforce the comfort that our cats find in ritualistic behaviour.*

BELOW *Once a cat has learnt to expect certain things at certain times of the day, he can become very persistent in demanding that the schedule be followed.*

OPPOSITE ABOVE *No accurate IQ tests have yet been devised to measure the intelligence behind those eyes. The language barrier will probably always stand in the way of such experiments.*

OPPOSITE BELOW *Ritual is an important aspect in any pet's life, and because they share their homes and lives with us our daily comings and goings will become essential parts of their rituals.*

This continued for several weeks, with the cat gaining enthusiasm for the game all the while. But when our friend was entertaining guests, she forgot all about the ritual. She and her husband removed the dinner dishes to the kitchen and returned with dessert. She then returned to the kitchen for a tray bearing a pot of coffee, eight cups, cream and sugar.

You've probably guessed by now what happened when she started from the kitchen into the dining room this time. Luckily, no-one was burned by the flying pot of hot coffee. The crockery didn't fare as well.

While these behaviours are often the source of amusement for us humans, they are just as deeply serious for our cats as the rituals of the wild were to their ancestors. Rituals bring much-needed order, comfort, security and a definite sense of a cat's place within its world. Once established, they must be observed.

CHAPTER FIVE

Is training worth attempting?

There is a gag in current use among many cartoonists that depicts a man and his cat in conversation. The man, very agitated, is saying something like "Fluffy, I'm really upset with you. That was a perfectly good plant. But look at what you did to it. It looks like some of your left-over food that's been sitting around for days." The cat, smiling and content, is actually hearing: "Fluffy, blah-blah-blah. Blah-blah-blah good blah. Blah. Blah-blah-blah food blah-blah-blah."

In other words, Fluffy is understanding only three words: "Fluffy", his name; "good", which the man usually uses to mean he is pleased with something that Fluffy has done; and "food", which Fluffy has learned means something good to eat. So the message that the cat is actually putting together from all this is, "Fluffy, good, food" – something quite different to what the man intended him to hear.

As exaggerated as this cartoon example may be, none of us who has lived with cats can deny the reality underlying it. This is not to say that cats cannot be trained, even to the point of performing tricks, just like dogs. Somewhere in the distant past, the idea arose of cats being totally different from dogs, and, we were told, because of this difference, we must expect them to respond less – if at all – to training. Perhaps both the cats and we humans would be better off if we didn't try to train them. The same false image of cats has led us to expect less affection, dependency and the like from them.

As with most myths about our domestic cats, this one begins with a certain amount of truth.

LEFT *Cats are unlike dogs in their behaviour because of millions of years of evolution into separate and distinct lifestyles. Somewhere, way back in pre-history, the canines and felines did share a common ancestor, however.*

Cats do not respond in the same way to training. Our approach must be entirely different from that we take in training other animals.

Dogs strive to learn your commands for little more than the security of having pleased their master – or, more correctly from the dog's perspective, the leader of their pack. Cats' motives are a bit more inner-directed (some might say downright self-centred).

The positive motivators in a cat's life are food, comfort (most often translated as warmth) and play/company. Negative motivators to a cat are wetness, discomfort (most often translated as anything but warmth) and loud noises.

PUNISHMENT AND REWARD

You'll notice that physical punishment, restraint or force does not find a place on either of our lists. This is because the reaction of most cats to such direct, purposeful contact is simple avoidance. "If you want to be that rough," the cat is telling you as it slinks quickly from the room, "I'll see you later." Perhaps the cat will respond in kind with claws and teeth to the first few physical efforts at discipline, but even this will soon be abandoned for retreat. Too many such encounters can leave a psychological imprint in the cat's mind against the "offending" human that can be nearly impossible to mend.

Even sharp verbal commands can have this effect. While a quick "No!" or "Stop!" will probably stop the cat from scratching at the furniture leg, too many of these will leave you with a nervous, retiring and shy animal.

When you yell at your cat, you are making a mental connection between your harsh command and whatever it is that you don't want the cat to be doing. But the cat forgets what it was doing immediately on hearing your sharp tone and instead identifies the discomfort with its source – you. For some reason which the animal cannot fathom, you are causing it discomfort.

This is the reason that so many animal behaviourists today recommend indirect deterrents to stop unwanted behaviour. A ball of paper or a short, gentle squirt from a water pistol have power equal to a harsh command in stopping the cat doing wrong, but the animal generally won't trace the source of its discomfort back to you. Consequently, you'll be able to repeat the deterrent as many times as necessary until the cat learns to cease the offending activity without your being identified as the bad guy.

A word of caution: even balls of paper and squirts of water can be carried too far, from the cat's perspective. In a sense, they are being delivered by some unseen enemy and constant, unexpected "attacks" can lead to a very nervous cat. Moderation is crucial. Take corrective measures only when absolutely necessary.

On the other hand, use the positive reinforcements as much as possible. Nothing perks up a

RIGHT *Patience, persistence and repetition are the prerequisites for developing any new forms of behaviour, or tricks, in your cat. As under wild conditions, the cat must come to recognize the benefits that the new behaviour holds for it.*

OPPOSITE *Food is one of the strongest motivators for our cats. Special treats can bring them to heights of performance.*

cat's attention span and memory capacity like a morsel of its favourite food, even more so if it's something that's not available every day.

For example, to teach the cat her name, hold a bit of the food out towards her and call her by name. If she comes, give her the food, speak in low, soothing tones of praise and pet or stroke her in whatever manner she most likes. Repeat this only a few times at a sitting to avoid losing the cat's attention and your patience, but try to do it at least once a day for a couple of weeks.

Many cat owners have followed this process using food at mealtime instead of the snack morsel. Each time they dished out the cat's meal, they

called her name and made a fuss of her when she came. At mealtime it's important that the training and praise do not interfere with the cat's eating or the opposite effect from that intended might be achieved.

Whatever training you choose to attempt with your cat and whatever successes you achieve, don't fool yourself that you've taught the cat the concepts of right and wrong. These are human words, without any true meaning for any other living creatures on earth.

Cats never feel remorse for any of their actions. They never feel accomplished because of what they have learned and performed. What they feel is their own current level of comfort and security. "Yeah, sure, I learned to do a triple somersault from the top of the shelves, catching my catnip mouse on the way down," they might say, if they could talk. "But how about dinner? Isn't it about that time?"

They will begin doing something and continue to do it only as long as they realize a direct benefit through the action. Conversely, they will cease

doing something and not do it again only as long as they realize a negative effect on themselves because of it.

Nevertheless, training your cat is a worthwhile pursuit, requiring extreme patience and understanding on your part. You must be willing to go back to the drawing board time and time again. But it will add a great deal to both your lives. The benefits that you might draw from a well-trained cat are obvious, but cats too gain from the training. They are highly inquisitive animals that will thrive on the stimulation that your efforts will provide for their minds. After all, sleeping for 18 hours per day doesn't provide much in the way of mind-bending challenges.

LAYING DOWN RULES OF BEHAVIOUR

Like his comic namesake, Garfield was a terror. Whether the effort to bring his behaviour into check had never been mounted or had simply been given up as of no use we never really knew. By the time we came across him, his furniture

ABOVE *Cats are very skilled and versatile at solving preoblems. Given enough time, this cat would have that mouse from under that glass cheese cover.*

LEFT *Some behaviour that we attribute to spite is actually the result of anxiety or boredom. Although cats spend large segments of time in sleep, they need some activity and distraction.*

shredding, drapery tearing and antagonistic attitude towards all visitors was pretty much taken for granted. His humans shared his home, and even provided his food and water, but otherwise he lived mostly independently of them.

To their credit, we never heard Garfield's humans mention getting rid of him as a solution to their mounting problem. It probably never even occurred to them. They are basically gentle souls, who honestly believe that animals have rights equal to humans and live their lives according to such principles.

On the other hand, they had done something of a disservice to Garfield by never enforcing any sense of what was acceptable and what was not. For the lack of a few strong words and perhaps a squirt or two of water in the early development of their cat-human relationship, they had allowed

the black Persian to grow into a cat that few people wanted to be around.

Cats need to be shown what is and what is not acceptable behaviour. Don't think for a moment that cats in the wild are not taught these valuable lessons by their mother, other cats and other animals. Survival depends upon the passing on and enforcement of certain "rules" from one generation to the next.

But when the cat is in a man-made environment, the situation changes in two very important ways. First, there are additional aspects that need to be incorporated into her behaviour so that she is an acceptable member of the household. Second, while nature generally relies much more heavily on negative teaching aids, the human teacher will be more successful when using positive reinforcement.

Reassuring a Nervous Cat

A cat should never be hit, not even the tiniest swat on the rump. Rather than taking this as an incentive to please you the next time, as the pack-loving dog might do, the cat only acknowledges and remembers the fact that you inflicted pain, no matter how minor.

If a cat backs off, probably either with its back arched in defensive posture or crouched in submission, it's likely that she has been abused by the hand at some time in her past. It's also possible that she has other reasons, learned and innate, for not liking the feel of a human hand on her, but abuse is always a first consideration.

With such a cat, you must earn her confidence before she will be comfortable with your stroking her. You must assure her, with your tone and with your motions, that she is in no danger from you. Don't expect instant acknowledgement.

To initiate touching with such a cat, very slowly and smoothly extend your flat hand along the floor in her direction. Don't make first contact. Stop your forward motion under her nose and wait for her to sniff your hand. Nothing about your movement should suggest to her that you intend to touch her, and make sure you don't betray that pledge by suddenly reaching for her. If she runs away, don't follow. Allow her some time alone, at least a half-hour or so, before trying once again.

OPPOSITE *This may be all the response that a "come" command draws from your cat, not because it doesn't understand the command but because it isn't choosing to obey just now.*

RIGHT *Your reaction to this situation could determine relations between you and your cat for the next several days. You want to dissuade such behaviour but not to the extent that the cat doesn't want to be near you.*

One negative enforcement that you will want to use is a loud, harsh "No!" Consistency in the use of this command whenever the cat is committing the unwanted behaviour is essential, although too much use of the word can lead to a nervous cat. Most cats will get the idea long before you've shouted too often.

Punishment must always come while the cat is engaged in the activity you want to curb. Telling the cat "no" after she has left the scene of the

ABOVE *Punishment of your cat should never include striking with the hand, or even the threat of striking. This can only cause the cat to view hands as a source of pain and discomfort.*

OPPOSITE *As cute and cuddly as any kitten may look, you're setting up your relationship with the cat for failure if you expect that there won't be some trying moments.*

LEFT *A typical cat response to chastisement is simply to hide from its source, unlike a dog which would attempt to seek forgiveness for whatever it had done wrong.*

scratched furniture and is eating from her bowl, even if you first carry her back to the furniture, sends some confusing signals. The scratching is in the past. It's already gone from the cat's mind. Why are you shouting at her for eating?

Beyond all forms of punishment, positive reinforcement will bring a cat over to your way of thinking much faster. Feline motivations are these: comfort, security, food and water. Pleasing you with her performance appears nowhere on that list, except as far as it is a means to accomplish one of these.

The first three are the most useful in trying to train a cat. A morsel of some favourite snack is

always welcome but gentle, soothing words and soft stroking are equally effective, because of their direct relationship in the mind of the cat to its comfort and security.

Your praise for everything the cat does correctly, even the smallest things, should be extreme and exaggerated. Punishment for those actions that you consider undesirable should move in the other direction. It should be reserved and restrained. You might even overlook some of the small problems.

Every breed of domestic cat and nearly every species of wild cat has been trained with these principles. Of course, different individuals have different capacities: some adapt much better to training than others.

When a new problem (or one that was previously corrected) surfaces in your cat, look for the underlying causes before you begin any corrective measures. Perhaps the inadvertent removal of the scratching post during housecleaning is the real reason for the recent attacks on the furniture. Replace the scratching post and the chances are good that the furniture-scratching will cease. Maybe you're not cleaning the litter box regularly enough and that's the cat's justification for turning elsewhere. Perhaps your cat is experiencing some new emotional stress or physical illness.

GRUDGES AND RESENTMENTS

Kaybee is fat by anyone's stretch of the imagination. Her belly drags on the floor when she walks to such a degree that she actually rubs fur from her underside. Her legs are bowed. Picking her up is no easy chore.

But in her mind, she's simply well-fed and maintained in the comfort to which she has become accustomed. Is it any wonder that she resents the efforts of our friend Pauline to enforce a bit of dieting?

That's right, she resents her reduced rations. Resents, as human as that emotion might sound, is the only word that's appropriate here. Kaybee has exchanged her previous greetings at the front door each evening with as purposeful a walk as she can manage in the opposite direction when Pauline gets home from work. She no longer "talks" to her in those little chats the two of them used to share.

As we write this, the diet's been under way for only a few weeks, so there's no way of knowing how far Kaybee will continue her grudge. She may very well come up with new ways to send her message to Pauline. Just as likely, she may call a halt to her protest over time.

Cats definitely hold grudges and feel resentment, although generally for much more basic and understandable reasons than we humans. Whenever they perceive a deprivation of some of the basic necessities that they've come to expect us to provide, they will register their complaints. They're just not as happy and contented as they were before, and it shows in their behaviour. That can mean anything from a simple lessening of enthusiasm to acts that might best be described as spiteful.

However, what at first appears to be an act of spite by a cat is more often than not motivated by anxiety or boredom. This is probably the underlying cause of Felix attacking the leg of the couch while you're out, even though he is normally happy to use the scratching post in the kitchen. He has no way of knowing how soon you intend

OPPOSITE *Rarely will cats be caught in the act of doing something that their owner has made clear is undesirable. This doesn't mean they won't continue the activity. They just won't get caught.*

RIGHT *Seeking the comfort and security that are the prime motivations in her life, your cat may try to avoid contact with you when she sees you as a disrupting force.*

to return. Maybe over the previous seven days you've been out for the same amount of time and Felix hasn't reacted to it. But, for whatever cat reason he may have, today he needed you close. When you weren't there his comfort and security levels dropped and anxiety built up within him, eventually finding this outlet.

WHO, ME?

You've probably noticed that whenever any indiscretions take place, catching the guilty party in the act (or even in the appearance of guilt) is just about impossible. For example, consider the shelf filled with favourite and fragile collectables that has also attracted the attentions of a cat for whatever reason – perhaps warm air collects there, perhaps there's a special feeling of security,

perhaps there is some other reason that you can't fathom. You've made it clear to the cat that the shelf is off-limits, and you never see the cat on it. However, as you approach that room you hear the "thud, thud" of a cat making its way down to the floor from some elevated position. As you enter the room, you see the cat seated on the floor, well away from the shelf, grooming. Sleepily he looks up at you, as if to say, "Oh, hello there. Fancy meeting you. I've just been sitting here on the floor for the past hour or so, grooming myself."

At times like these it's easy to believe in the concept of cat lies. Anyone who has spent much time at all around cats has at least one or two tales that seem to prove beyond a shadow of a doubt that cats do in fact tell lies, and quite often.

OPPOSITE *Our homes are a very strange world to our cats, filled with interesting things that we try to prevent them from touching. Such restrictions are quite artificial and foreign to the natural world.*

RIGHT *An action such as this that gives the cat a measure of reward can become difficult to curb if you don't react immediately and consistently.*

ABOVE *Our houseplants are a particular source of interest to our cats. They* *have a natural attraction to plants, and will claw and chew them.*

However, lying may be too human a concept for what the cats really are doing. You'll recall that comfort and security are among the chief motivators in the life of the cat. What better way for the animal to maintain some control over these areas than with secrecy about what it's been up to and where it's been doing it. The cat's philosophy here is this: "Nobody saw me, I didn't do it." The portrayal of innocence on your entry into the room may seem like plain dishonesty, but is, in fact another natural mechanism to avoid loss of comfort and security. If you didn't see the cat doing the forbidden action, there won't be any yelling or other punishments.

CHAPTER SIX

The
technological cat

In the Bill Murray movie *Scrooged* – a modernized version of Charles Dickens' classic tale *A Christmas Carol* – there is a subplot running through several scenes in which a television network executive wants mice incorporated into a Yuletide programme. His reasoning: Mice on the screen will attract and hold the attention of cats in millions of homes, who will in turn influence their owners to keep watching the programme. He envisages a day when entire channels will be devoted to cats.

Through several scenes in the movie, technicians try to work out just how to fit those mice into the show. The solutions range all the way to

OPPOSITE ABOVE *Cats adapt quickly to those of our technologies that fulfil their needs. Others they choose for the most part to ignore.*

OPPOSITE BELOW *Explanations of the how and why behind technology, such as our television sets, are not required by our cats. The boxes simply exist and sometimes things of interest come into the house through them.*

LEFT *Cats find the various pieces of technology with which we fill our homes to be interesting distractions from time to time, although from their own particular perspective. As with everything in their environment, our electronics are translated in terms meaningful to the cat's existence.*

stapling tiny antlers on the rodents to give them a Christmas "look".

The whole idea is played for humour, but how far off are the executive's ideas about cats and television? Novelty gift companies have recognized the possibilities in the fact that cats can differentiate images on the television screen and will spend time watching those that attract their attention. One American company sells a 30-minute "Kitty Video". The product is described as "Great fun for your cat (and you!) because it's shot from a cat's point of view." A black Persian is shown sitting in front of a television screen, tail twitching as it watches a bird hop invitingly along a log.

However, interest alone does not equal understanding. *America's Funniest Home Videos*, and the many imitations of that programme around the globe, have shown time and time again that seeing and reacting to something on the screen is not the same as understanding what is seen. Usually the cat comes off as looking foolish when it reaches for something on the screen with

its paw and falls from the top of the television cabinet or when it pounces on a television image and bumps into the screen.

From the cat's perspective, his sense of sight – and perhaps his sense of hearing too – has told him that there is some type of prey worth pouncing upon. Nothing in his experience has prepared him for the fact that his prey is no more than a one-dimensional collection of light rays – noth-

ing, that is, unless the cat has been taken in by this illusion several times previously.

You've probably known a cat or two that came running when the telephone rang. "Isn't that cute? He's answering the telephone," is the customary comment. But that completely misses the real point of why the ring of the telephone interests the cat.

Think, for a moment, about what happens when your telephone rings. You come to the phone, pick up the receiver and begin talking to whoever is calling. The cat has absolutely no way of knowing there is someone else at the other end of the telephone line listening to you. The natural and logical assumption for the cat is that you're talking to him – a pleasant experience – and the ring of the telephone caused you to do that. When you reach down and stroke him during the conversation, you're reinforcing the beliefs he already holds about the situation.

Danger Zones for Your Cat

To maintain a safe environment for your pet, watch out for potential hazards around the home, such as: (1) pans of boiling water or fat; (2) open stove doors; (3) trash cans harbouring bacteria and small fish bones; (4) boiling kettles; (5) sharp utensils; (6) household detergents; (7) open refrigerators; (8) open dryers or washing machines; (9) sockets and electrical cables which the cat may chew; (10) open doors leading onto high balconies; (11) objects resting precariously on table edges; (12) precarious ornaments on shelves; (13) fires with no fireguards; (14) poisonous houseplants; (15) drawers left open where the cat may become trapped; (16) young children or babies left alone in a room with a cat.

One of our first cats applied this same learning and reasoning mechanism to one of the other great cat motivators, food. Fed mostly a diet out of the can, Tabby soon came to identify the sound of the electric can opener with food. Taking it one step further, he reasoned that it was the sound of the small box that made one of the humans in the house get him some food. From there, it wasn't much of a stretch to discover that pressing down on one part of the small box produced the desired noise. In our typical "isn't that cute" approach, we were quick to reinforce the

OPPOSITE *Man's uses for something are of little consequence to our cats. Much more pertinent questions are: Can it make me feel more comfortable or secure? Can I eat it?*

RIGHT *There is a great deal in our homes to entertain and frustrate cats at the same time, such as these fish that can't be caught and eaten. Their movement is nevertheless fascinating.*

behaviour by praising Tabby, stroking him and – of course – giving him some food.

The downside of this misinterpretation of our technology is its potential for injury. The cat doesn't see the top of the engine in a car we've just driven as anything more than a dark, protected and, above all, warm place for a quick snooze. Many a cat has awakened just too late to avoid the engine's moving parts or a fall from a moving vehicle. An open clothes dryer presents much the same dangerous invitation for cats.

CAT'S EYE VIEW

In order to understand better your cat's non-human perception of all the technological marvels with which you've filled your home, stop for a moment and consider a few of them from a cat's point of view:

Refrigerator This is a good place. The humans often fetch tasty things to eat from inside it, although sometimes the food is colder than I like it. It's also a centre of activity every now and

OPPOSITE *A refrigerator is a vague concept for a cat, who sees it simply as a place where food comes from and therefore a good place to be.*

RIGHT *A great deal of warmth comes off our computers, providing the type of spot where our cat's comfort is very high. However, sleeping on computers should be discouraged because they emit large amounts of radiation.*

then, when they bring paper bags filled with food into the house and empty them into that thing . . . By the way, those paper bags make excellent hiding and play areas . . . I haven't yet worked out how to get in there myself.

Cupboard Another good place. This is where the humans kill my food every day before putting it in my bowl. I have found out how to get in there, but I haven't discovered any food myself, just round, shiny, hard things that often smell like lots of different foods but can't be bitten into.

Can opener The thing up there on the kitchen counter, where I'm not supposed to go, that makes a noise after the humans bring one of those round, shiny, hard things out of that place where they make the kill for my food and before they give me my food in my bowl.

Microwave oven Another thing that often makes noises before we eat. Food for my bowl usually doesn't come from here, but if I follow the humans after the noise has stopped, they're usually carrying something that I can share.

Garbage disposal, dishwasher, blender, food processor, etc. Something that makes a very loud noise near the place where the humans make the kills and the noise that signals dinner. It sounds dangerous and threatening, but it usually only makes the noise when the humans are nearby, so I'm not too frightened by it.

Vacuum cleaner Another noisy thing, but one that moves and will attack you if you get too close. The humans are always nearby when it is roaring, but I still prefer to leave the room. This thing really wrecks my comfort and security levels. Speaking of cleaning, I really hate that stuff the humans spray and rub on the furniture. It changes the smells of everything with which I'm familiar and makes me sneeze.

Television Other animals sometimes get into our home through this, without me ever hearing or smelling their approach. I've been chased by everything from a barking dog to a chattering monkey. Of course, sometimes I see things there that I want to capture. But those animals are difficult to grab and hold on to. They move about that thing, and come and go, very quickly.

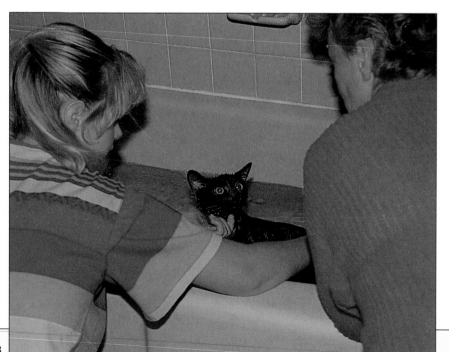

OPPOSITE *Cars hold a particular fascination for cats accustomed to the outdoors. They generally offer areas of warmth and elevation, two important criteria in every cat's comfort and security requirements.*

LEFT *Reactions differ from one cat to the next, but bathing is one concept that none of them will ever fully understand.*

Telephone Another noise-maker, but not one that really disturbs me. After it makes its noise, the humans usually appear and begin talking to me, which really helps boost my comfort and security levels.

Computer This is a non-threatening thing which the humans seem to spend a lot of time with during the day. When they're there, the top of that thing is a wonderfully warm place to sleep. [Because of the radiation that computers give off constantly, this practice should be discouraged in cats.]

Bath, shower The humans go there each morning and I hear water running. It's usually a warm place, but that darned water just won't leave me at ease there.

Sink Another place where I hear water running and one that I like even less than the other water-

place. Every now and then, the humans put me in this place, make me wet and rub something into my fur. It seems like forever before they stop all this and rub me with something that soaks a lot – but never enough of the water from my fur.

Doorbell A noise that signals someone is coming into our home. I never hear this noise before the humans who live here appear, so it means a stranger will enter. Some strangers are nice to be around. Some aren't.

Car Usually when I'm put into my kennel and taken outside I end up in this thing, which makes lots of noises and shakes and bumps quite a bit. Then I end up somewhere I really don't want to be, like the place where a human in a white coat puts me on a cold metal table and sticks me with sharp things or some place like my home but where everything is changed and different.

CHAPTER SEVEN

What shall I do with this dead mouse?

LEFT *An unrestrained, unsupervised cat can become the scourge of neighbourhood bird feeders, quickly earning the animal a bad reputation.*

BELOW *Even cats that are kept indoors for their entire lives will exhibit instinctive interest in prey species such as birds.*

Every owner of a cat that is successful in hunting mice, small birds, lizards and the like has at one time or another been presented with a specimen of one of these prey species. We greet the sight of these small trophies – dead, dying or quite lively – on our doorsteps, in our living rooms and on our beds with emotions ranging from revulsion to humour to pride. However, the emotion that would best suit us, as the freshly deposited mouse scurries under the couch, is a combination of shame, embarrassment and gratitude – at least from our cat's perspective.

Kitty has not brought the fresh catch of the day to your feet to gain your admiration, as is generally believed by cat owners. This act is in reality an insult of sorts, albeit unintended. Kitty – obviously adept in the skills of hunting – is bringing back the fruits of her labours to share with those who aren't as skilled.

The cat has interpreted your inability to catch mice, birds and the like on your own as a failing on your part. Like a queen teaching her kittens, Kitty is attempting to teach you the skills needed to be successful at the hunt. Failing that, she is

offering the food to you because you are incapable of feeding yourself.

As you can see, the rebuke or even punishment that Kitty often receives at this point sends some very mixed signals. She probably did not expect the cat equivalent of gratitude, but she definitely did not anticipate such a negative reception.

A much more thoughtful course for you at this point is to accept the prey, without much praise, excitement or concern. Then, when the cat's not

Your cat's activities while outdoors on its own can tell you something about the hunting abilities of its immediate parents and more distant ancestors. While there are many distinctions that can be made between mother cats in their relationships with their kittens, one of the most interesting is that between hunting and non-hunting females.

Does the female bring half-dead mice and other rodents back to the kittens for them to practise their hunting skills? Or does she go through all the motions of the hunt without ever making a capture or kill and, so, passes no complete hunting abilities onto the kitten?

next, and for carnivores like domestic cats obtaining food means hunting and killing prey.

Hunting is an instinctive behaviour in cats and often the most placid of them will display a near-devilish alter ego upon setting foot outdoors. Gone is the gentle, calm, retiring Fluffy of the inner sanctum. In her place, we suddenly find Sheba, killer cat of the jungle. Faster than you can snap your fingers, all of her wild instincts have come to the fore. She's a hunter, a defender of territory.

Although hunting is an instinct, bringing the hunt to a successful conclusion is something that must be learned. The skill involved in finding prey, stalking it, pouncing upon it, subduing it and killing it are normally taught by a mother to her kittens.

Lessons begin around the age of three weeks. At first the mother returns to the kittens with a dead prey animal, which she then eats in front of them. After a few such sessions, she switches to prey that is still alive, killing and eating it as the kittens watch. Next the queen presents live prey to the kittens for them to attack, kill and eat.

Graduation from this elementary school of hunting takes mother and kittens into the field. Here the skills are further demonstrated, refined

looking, dispose of it in an outdoor wastebin – as soon as possible, because rodents do carry a large population of parasites.

The sharing of the kill behaviour is most often noticed in female cats, probably because the responsibility of raising and teaching the young ones falls to them. The mechanisms for obtaining food are among the most important lessons that need to be passed from one generation to the

The Playful Predator

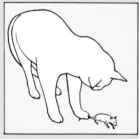

Why do cats torture their prey before they kill it? It does not occur to the cat that it is inflicting pain, for torture is not something it understands. The cat is simply releasing its pent-up hunting energies. The most common way of "playing" with a crippled victim is the shake. It is also commonly observed in dogs, and most other carnivorous predators. The reason for shaking the victim is obvious: a

violent shake or two will disorient any captured creature. It will upset the balancing mechanism of the ears. For vital seconds it will be unable to stand upright – and will certainly not be able to fight back or run away. Some cats hold down the prey with one or both forefeet, while they worry others. This behaviour may be related to the evolutionary past and the killing of snakes.

ABOVE *Waiting in ambush is a common part of the cat's style of hunting, which it often applies to play as well.*

and tested. A female in a territory that presents ample prey will generally be much more patient and forgiving with her kittens' mistakes and occasional reversions into play than will a female in a more prey-limited territory. This latter female may even take to cuffing inattentive kittens if prey is extremely scarce.

SIGNS OF THE HUNTER

Still not convinced that your sweet little cat, who never gets out of the house except under your constantly watchful eye, could be a hunter? The next time you're outdoors with her, watch for these telltale stages of hunting:

The wait: She sits on her haunches with her back very straight and her ears erect. Her tail may wave slowly from side to side. She is obviously scanning her surroundings, as her head turns very slowly and her ears quiver to take in every sound they can find.

The stalk: She drops down on all fours, crouched towards the ground with her legs slightly bent. Slowly, silently, cautiously, she moves in one direction, using every bit of cover that she encounters. After every few such steps, she drops her belly closer to the ground and sprints for a short distance.

The pause: She stops abruptly in whatever position she finds herself and stares with intensity at a spot ahead of her. This is probably the spot where she has sighted her prey. Then she will begin the stalk again, only to break off into another pause. This may be repeated several times.

The ambush: She stops, usually behind some bit of cover, and lowers her tense body to the ground. Her legs are ready to launch her at any moment. Every muscle is straining.

The pounce: She rockets forward from her last hiding spot until she is within striking distance.

She then lifts her front end from the ground, folding her front legs and paws under her chest momentarily, and launches herself forward.

The grab: She lands on her front paws. If she hasn't already pinned her prey to the ground, she'll make as many quick snatches at it as are

needed to complete this task. She then uses her paws to turn her prey for a death-bite, usually at the neck.

The kill: She bites the prey at the neck or rolls over on to her side, rakes her back claws against it and then delivers the death-bite.

Your particular cat may not perform all of these steps, which is generally an indication that she wasn't taught hunting/killing by her mother. These manoeuvres are mostly instinctive, but without that kittenhood education, the refinement just isn't there.

The step most often muffed by a poorly trained or untrained cat is the kill. Once such a cat has captured its prey it often doesn't know what to do with it. Of course, the most skilled mousers around have been known to "play" with their prey, releasing and recapturing it several times before finally making the kill or allowing a full escape. These cats are often seen tossing the prey into the air after they've captured it.

CAT WATCHING TIP

All cats hunt. Can yours kill? The answer to this question will tell you something about your cat's recent ancestry. Hunting mothers generally pass all their hunting abilities, including the ultimate killing of their prey, onto their kittens. Nonhunting mothers, by contrast, often pass along the hunting skills except the ability to kill. A cat's tendency to hunt or not to hunt will have been determined by its ancestors of several generations ago.

KITTY OLYMPICS

Cats are extraordinarily agile athletes. In addition to the hunting pounce discussed in this chapter, they have at least two other well-practised jumps in their repertoire: a carefully studied vertical leap and a spur-of-the-moment lunge when startled by an apparent threat.

The spur-of-the-moment lunge is almost self-explanatory. When a cat is suddenly frightened, a leap similar to the pounce will effectively launch it into a run for cover.

The vertical jump often appears to be the simplest act of impulse as the cat leaps up on to objects about the home, as much as five times above its own height. From a walk or trot, the cat just springs from the floor and lands squarely on its target. However, those nonchalant springs are actually performed from memory. The calculations were made, executed and tested previously. If the object were something new, you would see the cat stop for a bit and carefully plan the jump so that she flies well above the object. The return to the floor is often a less graceful, but neverthe-less well-planned, affair. The cat hangs as much of her front end over the edge as possible as a first step to decreasing the overall distance she must fall. She then pushes off with her hind legs. If she's coming down a considerable distance she will probably do it in a two-stage jump, first glancing off an intermediate object, even a wall, and pushing off from that with her hind legs to turn the fall into something which more closely resembles a horizontal leap.

If she's covered a considerable vertical distance, she will probably stop, shake her head and paws, and lick her paws. This is one moment when we get a false sense of some superiority over our cats. "A little higher than you thought?" is often our sarcastic remark at this time. Surprise, she knew what she was doing the whole time.

The facet of the cat's athletic prowess that is most widely known and admired is something

OPPOSITE ABOVE *Domestic cats are able to leap at least five times their own height, placing many supposedly protected objects within their reach.*

OPPOSITE BELOW *Squirrels and birds attracted to a windowsill by the offering of nuts and seeds provide plenty of diversion for a house-bound cat throughout the day.*

RIGHT *Cats generally land with deft precision because they have spent time planning every jump before actually trying it.*

Nine Lives

"Cats always land on their feet." This old saying is almost always true, for the animal will make every effort to do so. This picture sequence shows the cat using its tail to right itself while still in mid-air, and make the landing squarely on its feet, so that its powerful legs will absorb the shock.

BELOW *It is a myth that falling cats always land on their feet, but they have an inner ear mechanism that improves their chances of pulling it off.*

called the righting reflex. This is the cat's ability to turn its body as it falls, righting itself before hitting the ground or floor.

It's commonly thought that a falling cat will always land on its feet. More often than not the cat will perform the manoeuvre successfully, but we have seen them smack the floor on their backs and sides hard enough to hear the air knocked out of them. Even cats encounter circumstances now and again that they can't control.

An inner ear mechanism known as the vestibular apparatus is responsible for the righting reflex. This apparatus is a series of fluid-filled chambers lined with millions of small hairs. Any movement of the hairs is relayed instantly to the brain, the direction of the movement revealing the position of the head. The brain immediately sends the signal to turn the cat's neck muscles so that the head moves to an upright position. The rest of the body follows as resulting signals are sent along the spinal column. This all takes place in the wink of an eye.

CHAPTER EIGHT

People who don't like cats – and vice-versa

bananas

Have you ever noticed that cats seem to be attracted to the one person in the room who hates them?

We've all heard, and probably believed, the old wives' tale that cats positively enjoy foisting themselves upon those humans who are silly enough not to like them. We believe this misconception has perpetuated itself among cat-lovers for so long because it represents a sort of sublime revenge upon cat-haters.

The observation behind the statement is absolutely correct. It is proven again thousands of times each day by cats and cat-haters around the world. You can test it out yourself, if you want. All it takes is an invitation to a friend who is a known non-cat person.

However, the inference that has been drawn from the observation is faulty. The real attraction for the cat is the area immediately around the non-cat person.

Picture a room filled with seated people enjoying a party. As the cat walks through territory that he normally shares with only a certain few select humans, nearly every person tries to touch him. Some even try to pick him up. It's an unnerving experience at best, one that goes against all the basics of comfort and security that he seeks to keep firmly in his life at all times.

Then he happens to pass by the non-cat person. Wait, he thinks, no-one is trying to molest me at this spot. Perhaps this is a safe haven. Several minutes later, because no-one has yet assaulted him there, the cat is curled up against the feet of the non-cat person, who is often rather uncomfortable by this time.

There are, of course, some reasons for not liking cats. The fear of cats (ailurophobia) is a very real phobia for those rare individuals thus afflicted. Some people suffer from an overall fear of animals, another psychologically treatable phobia. Alternatively, the person simply may not like animals. He may not have been raised with them in the home. He may genuinely not feel the need for the many gifts that animals bring into the lives of their humans.

Perhaps the visitor's dislike of cats is more superficial. Maybe he simply doesn't like the arrogant image of the cat that has arisen from

OPPOSITE *To the non-cat person this is how the home with one or more cats may appear on approach.*

LEFT *On the other hand, this is how the cat that doesn't like company may feel when that person enters her home. Is he gone yet?*

popular misconception, or maybe he's heard of human health concerns that relate to cats. Maybe there's a bad experience with a cat in his background, not severe enough to cause a phobia but enough to put him off the animals.

Whatever the reason, as a good host you must walk a tightrope between satisfying a guest and maintaining the bond that you've built with your cat. Since Kitty was looking for sanctuary in the first place when she settled against his feet, maybe she would be accepting of a little help in finding that peace in another room. She shouldn't be shooed from the room – instead, pick her up gently, talk to her lovingly and walk slowly into the new room. Once there, a few minutes more of your time with her is a good investment.

THE DYSFUNCTIONAL CAT

With some cats this situation will probably never arise. With them the dislike is not one-sided, for there are those felines who just can't abide us humans and our strange ways. They prefer to give us all, or all but a special human or two, as wide a berth as they possibly can.

"Oh, that's just crazy Snowball being herself," isn't an adequate explanation for your cat's explosive escape when someone new is visiting the house. Your visitor may think they are seeing a terrified animal, and terrified animals naturally have some reason for being terrified. Could it be beating and abuse?

Running and hiding from humans may in fact be one symptom of what is technically known as unhabituated anxiety. In layman's terms this means the cat has a built-in increasing nervousness about its inadequate knowledge of the world around it. This generally begins in a kitten that just doesn't experience enough different situations in its early, formative weeks and months.

Some kittens aren't as outgoing as their siblings and thus miss out on many of the normal life-preparing experiences. These kittens grow into noticeably less aggressive, even overly submissive, cats. They generally also display noticeably fewer

ABOVE *Some cats are very vocal in their displeasure at the approach of new humans. These cats want to meet life on their own terms and in their own time.*

OPPOSITE *Cats that have been raised with much positive handling from their first days of life are likely to be very receptive to contact with humans, including those with whom they aren't familiar.*

RIGHT *Others will simply slink off into a corner to wait for the current invasion of their home to come to an end and things to return to normal.*

skills in most of the "higher" cat functions, such as hunting and parenting.

In some sense, these cats also realize that they lack basic skills needed to deal successfully and aggressively with the world. This is where the escape and hiding response enters into their repertoire. In effect it is their way of dealing with a world that they can't otherwise handle. If they vacate the situation, if they remove themselves from the line of sight, they won't be drawing attention to their many shortcomings and exposing themselves to potential attack.

At these times, the apparently compassionate action of trying to draw the cat out of hiding to comfort it is exactly what the cat is trying to escape. Suddenly it is the centre of attention. It is no wonder that the feline lashes out with her claws in what she sees as a last, small effort to hide her inabilities.

Each effort to "help" Snowball under such circumstances will generally serve to convince her that her actions are correct, only she needs to find a more secure hiding place. The behaviour will become a bigger part of her life. She will spend

OPPOSITE *Often there is a very good reason why cats don't like to have company in the home. Rough handling at some time in the past is one obvious cause of this.*

LEFT *Many cats form special affections for certain members of the family. Only occasionally does this special bond occur to the total exclusion of all others.*

more time trying to perfect the technique. And because we humans generally tend to give in to situations like this fairly quickly, our actions will further convince her that she has come up with a successful mechanism for survival. She can only get worse under this scenario.

THERAPY

These dysfunctional cats can be helped to some extent, although just how balanced they can ever become remains highly variable from one cat to the next. The most helpful response that we can make to this fright and flight syndrome is to force the cat to remain in the situation that she wants to flee. By carefully gently and gradually forcing the cat to see that the terror that she imagined does not exist, we can make her less sensitive and fearful of the situation.

Don't hold the cat yourself to restrain her from running – this only serves to give her something else to fear. You may even put yourself into the role of villain or enemy. Plus, you'll probably end up with some painful claw marks on your hands and arms.

Instead, place the cat in a kennel that she is accustomed to and generally accepts as a secure, safe place. Put fresh water and food and comfortable bedding – the things that the cat knows she needs to lead a comfortable, secure life – into the kennel, which should be located somewhere out of the way in the room your visitor will be in.

At first, make the cat stay in the room for only a few minutes. No-one should make a fuss over her – it's best not even to acknowledge her presence. After a few minutes, carry the kennel and cat into another room, talking to her in gentle, soothing tones as you do. Leave her there, in the kennel, alone.

If the visit is going to last more than a half-hour or so, return to the kennel – alone – at about that time and open the door, again talking to the cat in gentle, soothing tones. Leave her there and return to your visitor in the other room.

Repeat this procedure several times, increasing the amount of time that the cat remains in the room where the visitor is located by a few minutes each time. When the cat finally begins to

OPPOSITE *A restrictive enclosure, such as a travel kennel, may be needed to get some cats past their fright-and-flight reaction to visitors.*

BELOW *A protected place in the room where we spend most of our time with visitors, off-limits to everyone but the cat, may encourage him to remain in the room rather than look for other cover.*

Handle with Care

The correct way to pick up a cat. (1) Place one hand under its front legs and the other under the hind quarters. (2) Keep one hand firmly under the hind quarters, supporting the cat's full weight. (3) Hold the cat upright, with one hand round its upper chest for support.

exhibit less anxiety over a visitor, try opening the door of the kennel while it is still in the same room, after the first few minutes. At this point, no-one should make a fuss over the animal.

Generally, Snowball will tell you when she is ready to face the experience without the comfort of her sanctuary. She will emerge from the kennel on her own. If she leaves the room without running or hunching over and almost crawling away, you're making progress. Continue with the procedure, cautioning visitors in advance not to make a fuss over her.

LEARNING TO ACCEPT HANDLING

An even less desirable reaction to human contact is the petting-attack response. This can range from an arched back and a hiss all the way to full-scale assault with claws and teeth. It generally signals a cat that has some stressful experience connected with a human in its background.

Being petted and held are not natural experiences for the cat. In the natural state, about the closest that a cat might come would be some social grooming with other cats, using only the tongues, or some greeting rituals.

These human things that we want to do with our cats must be learned. And, as with everything else we want to teach our cats, different cats will be more or less successful in learning them.

Some cats will be further along in the process than others when they join the household in which

ABOVE *Of course, there are those cats who are never going to get over their negative reaction to contact with unfamiliar humans. Sometimes we just have to accept this about them.*

OPPOSITE *On the other hand, some cats welcome the infusion of new activity, new smells and so on that visitors bring into their home.*

they are to live. Those who spent their first weeks of life as kittens being handled often but gently and were then placed in their new home shortly after being weaned (six to eight weeks of age) are more favourably inclined towards all handling. However, even among such litters there will usually be one or two kittens that aren't as outgoing and socialized as their brothers and sisters.

In addition, there are many anti-contact cats whose negative attitude towards being held or stroked can be traced to a few bad experiences after their initial socialization. Only patience, persistency and gentleness will bring these cats around – to the extent that they can be brought around at all. Those who have the bad experience too firmly etched into their minds may never be the cuddling cat that we all hope for in our companion animals.

To begin training a cat to the hand, so to speak, remember: petting is a much simpler concept that aligns much more comfortably with the natural order of social contact among cats. A few gentle strokes are usually enough to convince the cat that this can be pleasant experience.

Being picked up, on the other hand, is a totally foreign, and even threatening, occurrence. In the natural, wild state, it is only enemies who attempt to pick up an adult cat. Gradual and gentle actions that give the cat a sense of support and stability are essential as you introduce the new activity. Although the cat should be returned to the floor at the first sign of real discomfort, it should not be allowed to jump from your arms. This not only adds an unnecessary element of stress as the cat falls to the floor, but at the same time reinforces unacceptable behaviour.

CHAPTER NINE

Food,
glorious food

One of the most widespread bits of misinformation about domestic cats is the myth of the finicky cat. While individual cats most certainly do possess and regularly demonstrate their preferences for one type of food over another, much of this picky behaviour – probably much more than can ever be proved conclusively – relates to the quality of the food rather than the type. By quality we're referring to the taste and smell of the food when it's served rather than the original ingredients that went into it.

Exactly how strong and how important the cat's sense of smell really is has not yet been determined with any certainty. It is safe, however, to place it somewhere well above our own but still below that of the dog. In its simplest terms, this means cats can smell a great many more things about their food than we can.

Of course, it goes almost without saying that spoiled or spoiling food will curtail even the heartiest of appetites, but this question of quality cuts much deeper than that. Maybe the chemical of the plastic bowl is slowly leaching its way into the atmosphere, releasing some pretty strong and repulsive odours, at least to the more sensitive nostrils of the cat. Perhaps the smell of the chemical cleansers used to wash the bowl still linger, under the magnified inspection of a cat's nose. Or maybe the bowl hasn't been cleansed sufficiently to remove the rotting smell of a meal that the cat already turned down a couple of days earlier in the week.

Although this is not a book about cat health and diet, it seems appropriate to add a cautionary note at this point: *cats are carnivores; they need meat to survive in health.* The animal rights anti-meat lobby has tried to convince us that our pets can get by just fine on a totally vegetarian diet. This may be true for dogs (although we're never going to eliminate the excitement that they feel over a piece of meat) but it most definitely is not true for cats. A diet completely lacking in any meat is

LEFT *A secluded, out-of-the-way spot for dining is a great comfort to your cat, allowing for relaxed and unhurried eating.*

The Rib Test

The rib test remains a reasonably effective guide to whether or not a cat's weight is correct. If you cannot feel each rib individually, without exerting undue pressure, then the cat is probably too fat. If the ridges of the cat's ribs feel like pencils, the chances are that it is not being fed enough, or that it is suffering from a condition which needs immediate attention from your vet.

more than likely depriving the cat of some nutrients that are only available from animal flesh, such as the arachidonic fatty acids and ready-to-use vitamin A.

Another contributing factor to the feeding problems of a cat that has been termed a finicky eater may be environmental. Feeding is a time when an animal's guard is temporarily let down. Therefore, eating is most comfortably enjoyed in quiet, seclusion and security. Feeding bowls placed in high traffic areas of the home obviously do not meet these criteria.

THE FAT CAT

Obesity is a very real problem in our cats – indeed, it's a problem for nearly all species of animal that are kept as domestic pets. We humans in the developed world have shared this failing with our companion animals!

A true definition of an overweight cat is hard to come by. We've discussed this subject with several different veterinarians and heard nearly as many different opinions. Society's view of feline obesity seems to be in a constant state of change. Also, some breeds carry their weight less obviously than others. Although some experts would go further with their definitions, your cat is probably fat if you can't feel her ribs without applying more pressure than you do when stroking her.

Sometimes excess weight can be attributed to a cat's physiology, but more often it is the result of a personality quirk – there are some cats that will eat to excess whenever they get the chance.

Of course, even these cats need human assistance to eat their way to an overweight state. Food left in the bowl all day encourages the cat to eat just as an open box of chocolates sitting on the end table while we watch television tempts us. No cat needs food to be available throughout the day. Two meals should be provided, and no more.

If you're already feeding at the proper rate, perhaps you should consider a switch to a higher quality food. Advertising claims to the contrary, some commercially available foods are packed with fillers and starches that are of little use to the cat's body, except when it comes to putting on

OPPOSITE *Cats have a fondness for milk and will go to great lengths to get it. However, some of them also have allergies to it or difficulty in digesting it.*

BELOW *Preventing behaviour that some people find offensive can often be simple. In this case, shutting the toilet lid and providing an alternative water source would probably solve the problem.*

excess weight. In the past few years some new brands have emerged that provide the ultimate balanced diet. These are generally not available on grocers' shelves, but a trip to the pet shop is worth while for the potential weight-loss in your cat.

Another reason for a fat cat is lack of sufficient daily exercise. Cats are natural-born slackers when it comes to physical exertion, and they certainly don't worry about their waistlines. They need some additional incentive to get moving.

You can provide that added motivation. You probably know your cat's favourite form of play. Engage him in games for as long as his interest holds. You can also up the frequency of your play periods. If you play with him for 15 minutes every other day or so, change to 15 minutes every day. If you already play for 15 minutes every day, perhaps you could find another quarter-hour elsewhere in the day for a separate session.

Scavenging

It has been said by certain theorists that to a cat no meal is really worth the eating unless it has involved the eater in at least some token effort to beg, steal or hunt. Certainly, even the fattest of domestic cats will go to considerable trouble to steal, even if it is merely knocking down and ripping open a box of its own dried catfood to win the unambitious reward of a few illicit morsels.

CHAPTER TEN

Coping with sickness and stress

M ost of us have heard of the elephants' graveyard, that mythical place where all elephants go to die. The legend could just as easily have been developed about a cats' graveyard. There would be as much truth to the latter notion as the former.

Such mass graveyards, filled with the bones of hundreds of thousands of one species, do not actually exist, except in the form of human cemeteries. However, it's easy to understand how such a myth arose.

The animal response to pain and illness is different to the human one. Animals' first instinct is not to seek out help, comfort and relief from others of their kind, or from human housemates in the case of our cats. They don't have our scientific understanding of what's really amiss under these circumstances. Instead, they are left to their own analysis of the situation. And what they

ABOVE *Cats find many ways of telling us what they want us to do and what they don't want us to do. Such as, "Do you really have to leave on this business trip?"*

perceive the pain or discomfort to be is the result of a sudden attack by some enemy, invisible though that enemy might be.

In the face of such an attack, the reasonable animal behaviour is to escape and hide. The most secure hiding place in the cat's territory is generally selected as a refuge.

Cats that are allowed to roam freely outdoors and are familiar with a much larger territory often just seem to vanish, never to return. Rather than running away, as is commonly assumed, many of these cats have simply curled up and died in some vacant building or stack of rubbish.

During episodes of illness, compassion from a human is rather meaningless while the pain or discomfort goes right on attacking. The one

exception may be the cat that has been conditioned to view a human's lap or arms as packed with security and comfort.

The sudden absence of a cat from its normal "rounds" about the house may therefore be among the very first symptoms of injury or illness. As we've explained elsewhere in this book, there can be other reasons for a reclusive cat, but if the change in routine comes on suddenly a trip to the vet may be in order.

SOURCES OF STRESS

Injury and illness are just two of the many things that we take for granted in our everyday lives which pose great mysteries to our cats. However, much of the human environment will be accepted or even used to their own advantage by cats (see Chapter 6), although they don't understand the purposes that we humans originally intended.

Other aspects of this strange human world will continue to baffle the cat throughout its life. The sudden change in attitude towards the cat's use of furniture when a new living-room suite is brought into the house is beyond Kitty's comprehension. It's not that difficult to understand her reaction of avoiding the living room and possibly her humans, who seem to have gone insane and are suddenly scolding for activities that yesterday were perfectly acceptable. The new furniture represents nothing more than the loss of much beloved, familiar territory to Kitty. She just doesn't have the capacity to understand or share your excitement about this acquisition.

Similar reactions can arise to nearly anything new that we bring into the cat's territory, which coincidentally is also our home. New babies, new pets, rearranged furniture all represent change, and often change accompanied by new attitudes on our part. Moving to a new house is probably the change with maximum impact on the cat, who sees only the loss of familiar territory and a massive need for readjustment.

Another source of cat stress is being forced to spend excessive time alone. This is not widely recognized because of the independent nature of our cats in comparison to other companion animals. It's true that cats are not pack animals but they do need social contact, with other cats where possible or with their human housemates as a substitute.

Any absence longer than a normal workday, if repeated regularly, is probably enough to cause some degree of loneliness in most cats. Those cat owners who find themselves out of the house for such extended periods may want to bring a second

cat into the home, being careful that the two felines are compatible with one another.

Many aspects of the man-made world into which we bring our cats can cause them stress, although the amount of stress and the reaction to it will vary from one cat to the next. Just like humans, cats vary in their capacity to deal with stressful situations. And, just as in humans, stress can lead to illness in our cats.

Early symptoms of stress can include drastic changes in normal daily activity, increased amounts of time spent in self-grooming, loss of or increase in appetite, change in the condition of the coat and dullness in the eyes. These, of course, are the early symptoms for a great many cat ailments, so home diagnosis is not practical. If a few such symptoms show up and cannot be explained through your observations on your cat, a visit to the veterinarian is in order.

Many of these same symptoms will be noticed in a depressed cat. Don't get us wrong – we're not advocates of the pet psychologist trade that caters to the animals of the rich and trendy. But we are convinced that animals, especially sensitive ones like our cats, do feel a sense of loss when

OPPOSITE *Cats also do not understand our attempts to heal them. Splints and bandages such as those on this kitten's leg are seen as something restrictive and often as an invasion of their body.*

RIGHT *The loss of some member of the household, whether through death or simply because they moved away from home, can send some cats into depression.*

someone leaves their lives and they do experience a form of depression over that loss. In other words, cats mourn.

They also have many more occasions to mourn than humans do. We've never seen any evidence to point to the fact that cats understand the concept of death, but loss is another thing entirely.

The cat feels loss whenever someone from its familiar world is no longer there. This interferes with its feelings of comfort and security, and the cat is therefore anxious about the change.

Death of a family member – and this description includes other pets that share the home – is one reason for loss, but to the cat it is the same when

OPPOSITE *Repeated searches may be conducted for any member of the family who is gone for a longer than normal period.*

LEFT *Sometimes the addition of a new family member can snap a mourning cat out of its depression over the loss of a previous member.*

a teenager goes off to college or when the family is broken by divorce. Even something as temporary as a member of the family away for vacation or on an extended business trip has been known to trigger this mourning response in some cats. The fact that the missing individual will be resurfacing from time to time just isn't in the cat's frame of reference.

Kitty's first reaction will be several thorough searches of the home for the missing individual over the first few days of separation. Often, these investigations are accompanied with a regular series of questioning meows.

The next step will usually be a period of sulky, sluggish behaviour. The cat will have lost just about all of her normal appetite for play, quite possibly for food as well. She'll spend much more time than normal just lying about, not in sleep but in apparent boredom.

At this point, intervention is suggested to prevent the more severe symptoms. Perhaps the cat's focus on the lost companion can be broken with the introduction of a new member to the family. If your conditions permit, this is often an excellent time to introduce a second cat to the home. Having more people over to the house can also help to fill the void.

Also, you might try to "jump-start" Kitty out of her malaise. Add some variety to her life by introducing some new games, particularly exciting games of the ambush variety. Try some new toys, and follow the guidelines in the next chapter to make those toys all the more appealing to her. Think up something new to add to her dinner menu. Allow her a few extra sessions with the catnip (see pages 133-5).

Do anything you can think of to divert the cat's attention from the loss she is feeling. Make certain that all other things that relate to her levels of comfort and security are maintained, and, if possible, enhanced.

Animals have relatively short attention spans, so you should be able to fill her life so full that she can't help but snap out of it before too long.

CHAPTER ELEVEN

The pleasures
of play

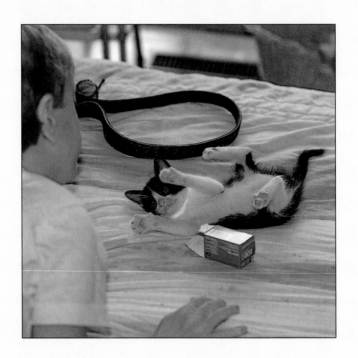

Adult visitors to Gramma's home would smile in disbelief at stories of the rambunctious antics of Quincy – at least those who visited without children in tow. There was simply no way that they could accept such tales about the pleasingly plump calico. The only Quincy they had ever seen was a placid, retiring cat that did little beyond lie on Gramma's lap and stretch and yawn occasionally. To them that was the only personality that Quincy exhibited. Even the basketful of cat toys, from rubber milk bottles to catnip-filled cloth mice, that Gramma had collected for him never seemed to attract more than a passing glance.

But in the presence of children a completely different cat emerged. A roughhousing, fleet-footed, even lovingly aggressive fool of a cat occupied Quincy's mind and body whenever young playmates were available. Every conceivable game seemed to come immediately to mind, from ankle-attack tag to all-out wrestling, the rougher the better.

The one trait that Quincy seemed able to carry into either of his personalities was that of gentleness. No matter how rough the play might become, Quincy never used his claws or teeth.

While such a completely split personality is not at all common in cats – at least not when it comes to play – much else among the attitudes that Quincy exhibited can be generalized across domestic cats as a whole.

Cats love to play. They even show much originality in the play they invent, such as stalking a spot of light on the wall, and in attracting us to take part with them. But they also have some pretty strong rules about their play.

LEFT *One of the most important criteria in play for cats is near-constant motion. Expensive toys are not necessary to provide this.*

All but the most malfunctioning kittens need play. It's the primary means of learning the early lessons about how to survive as a cat. Even kittens of wild cats, from the bobcat to the African lion, spend much of their early weeks in play. Those kittens that are too weak or sick or otherwise unable to engage in the full extent of play with their siblings will have a much tougher time of it throughout their lives.

Most cats carry some of the playful instinct with them into adulthood. They even continue to need the activity, particularly those that are cooped up all day by themselves in small apartments or even large houses. For these "home alone" cats, the play period that follows the arrival of the humans in the late afternoon and evening is a special time. The activity contributes not only some vital exercise, but also an opportunity for bonding and growing closer. Even roughhouse play, if your cat has demonstrated a liking for it, will serve this purpose.

Laid out like this in print, such set-aside playtime may sound like an overly taxing drain on your crucial time after a hectic day at the office, but just 10 or 15 minutes is a long time for your cat. Wouldn't such a brief respite be a pleasant way for you to wind down as well?

PROVIDING PLAY

Movement is the critical aspect in cat play. If it's moving, the cat's interested. This explains why the hundreds of dollars'-worth of toys scattered about the house just don't seem to provide an adequate substitute for your hand or foot. Those toys do nothing on their own. They just lie there. You're the energy behind any of the interesting motions they manage.

Think like a mouse. The little rodent scurries as fast as it can from one bit of cover to the next, stopping at each to peer out nervously before starting again on its fleeting way. This is the type of movement that cats most enjoy.

They also enjoy the pounce and capture, which is the ultimate goal of any hunt (now replaced with play). If the cat manages to catch and chew on the mouse (toy) every so often during the play period, his interest will be maintained for considerably longer.

In the wild state, much of the play behaviour of a cat will disappear with maturity. The regular pursuit of enough prey to survive and continue the species brings a much more serious aspect to the whole affair, not to mention the constant attention to avoiding dangerous enemies.

However, in your house most of these worries have been eliminated, which influences your cat's continued interest in play for two reasons. First, by providing nearly all of the cat's food, you are assuming the role of a parent cat and allowing your feline to retain much of its kitten-ness into and through adulthood. Secondly, it is as well to accept that the hunting instinct never dies and that the well-adjusted cat must find some new routes into which it can channel all the energy that would normally be directed in this manner. Active play is the perfect substitute.

OPPOSITE *New places to explore, regardless of how simple and commonplace, are like amusement park rides to our cats. Don't miss the opportunity to give a box or bag to your cat.*

RIGHT *Some play is more welcome than others, as this kitten may learn soon after dropping on the sleeping adult.*

ABOVE *Sometimes it seems that cats hate to be caught in the midst of some ridiculous action. The truth is that they are generally waiting to determine what your response will be.*

OPPOSITE *Cats are inventors of their own activities. Some are better at it than others, but we should always feel special when a cat sees fit to share a new game with us.*

LEFT *Play is a natural thing for kittens, and should be encouraged throughout the life of all cats. It keeps their minds active and their bodies in shape.*

There are some common cat games that will interest almost any feline. The clichéd activities such as batting at a suspended ball of yarn have become clichéd because so many million cats have perpetuated them down through the generations. Hide and seek, with either you or your Quincy hiding and then ambushing the other as he walks by, is also a standard.

Every cat and owner will also invent their own special play. Remain open to each new opportunity that presents itself during play period and you'll find yourself and your cat doing just that. It's likely that whatever little games the cat comes up with will be clues to what it enjoys most.

Blanket chase, where the owner's hand is attacked while moving beneath a blanket, rug, towel or some similarly soft covering, will entice even sedentary felines. Hide the toy, in which some of the cat's favourite possessions are hidden about the house, will play upon the natural feline curiosity. This is a particularly good game for you to set up for the cat before leaving for work each morning.

These are some of the games that have proven most enjoyable with the majority of cats we've owned or known, but they are only a starting point and not an all-inclusive list. The important aspect of cat play is not form but motion.

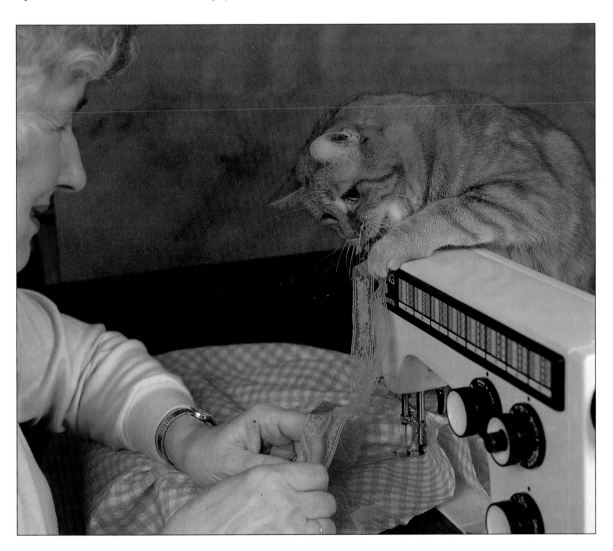

CHAPTER TWELVE

Facing the great outdoors

uphrates is a blue bi-colour Sphynx, who, to the best of our knowledge, has never experienced the outdoors except when transported in her kennel from one indoor location to the next. This is probably the way it should be. The Sphynx is a man-made breed, refined since 1966 for its hairless quality. Even the slightest draught on an otherwise warm summer's day can send these cats into spasms of shivers.

To owners of many other breeds and the ever-hardy moggies this may sound cruel indeed. But Euphrates, and other cats like her, probably has

ABOVE *Cats that have experienced the outdoors generally have a longing to return there again and again, if only for very brief periods at a time.*

LEFT *Some cats genuinely have no desire ever to leave the comfort and security of their homes. The attraction of new sights and sounds just doesn't pull as strongly on them.*

never even thought of the possibility of some world beyond the one she shares with her humans.

The outdoor world would be a terrifying, hostile place, filled with things she didn't understand and had never encountered before. Her personality really could not cope with it all.

And, if temperatures dipped from those of a very warm day, she would have a hard time dealing with it physically, as well.

She doesn't know she's missing anything and, given her delicate nature, quite probably she isn't. Cats that have never experienced life in the outdoors generally don't feel any need for it. They've built their entire lives around the world that they find within the safe and secure walls of their home.

On the other hand, a cat who has got the feel of the outdoors will probably always have some need for an occasional return there. Like all living things, cats who aren't restricted by some special circumstances generally do enjoy a change of scenery and some fresh air. It's still a new concept – one that is often met with ridicule and disagreement – that cats can be taken for a walk like dogs.

The big difference is that cats are more prone to resist the mechanisms involved in taking that walk than their canine counterparts. As with everything you want to teach to your cat, remember that he is motivated mostly by his own needs and wants rather than what you want for him. Unlike a dog, he's not going to submit readily to collar and leash simply because it will make you happy.

He needs to see the direct benefits early in the process to warm up to the idea of having any form of restraint placed on him. Here is where a Catch 22 situation takes shape. You shouldn't really allow your cat outdoors without that restraint, but he's going to resist that restraint until he's seen the wonders of the outdoors.

Many members of the cat fancy solve this problem by never addressing it. They simply allow the cat outdoors alone or under constant observation. This is unfair to many cats who are not equipped to deal with all the dangers of the outdoors, both natural and man-made. Even the most carefully watched cat will easily escape from his intended area of roaming if he wants. Commands to come back will likely fall on deaf ears.

That said, clearly some cats will adapt far better to the great outdoors than others, and their territorial environment will itself vary greatly: from urban sprawl to rural farmland. Use discretion, therefore, but bear in mind that nearly all cats can

OPPOSITE *A harness does not have the threatening feel about the neck that a collar can impart.*

RIGHT *Contrary to popular misbelief, cats can be taught to walk at the end of a leash. Some come to enjoy the experience.*

be taught to walk on a leash, given enough time and patience on the part of the teacher.

LEARNING TO WALK ON THE LEASH

As a first step, a soft but sturdy harness needs to be chosen. (A harness is better than a collar because it is less threatening to the cat psyche than a stranglehold.) The cat's natural curiosity is your biggest ally at this point. Toss the harness on the floor, near (not in) the cat's bed, and leave it there for several days. This will give the cat a chance to examine the harness on its own terms and to accept it as just another piece of the house.

When he seems to be comfortable with the harness and is no longer purposefully walking around it, try slipping it over his head during a play period. Continue to talk to the cat in a normal voice. If he accepts the harness, heap his favourite praise on him. Remove the harness gently, again with praise, after just a few minutes.

OPPOSITE *The outdoors offers additional exercise that can bring variety to the cat's life while helping him to stay fit.*

LEFT *Being trained to the leash allows your cat to go safely into fairly built-up areas under your control.*

If he rejects it, go back to playing for another few minutes, then try it again. If he rejects it again, forget it for that day. Never force him to submit to the harness. Try again the next day, adding a few morsels of his favourite snack as you are placing the harness over his head.

Repeat the process again the next day, leaving the harness over his head for several minutes longer. Next day try a longer period and so on, for a week or more.

Next try the process with the addition of fastening the under-belly strap of the harness. Many cats, by this time, won't be put off by the additional restraint but if yours is annoyed by the concept, remove the harness immediately and gently. Try again the next day.

After several days of wearing the full harness, the cat should be ready for the leash. Snap it to the harness, pick up your end and allow the cat to lead wherever he wants. You don't want to give the impression that you are somehow threatening the cat, or you'll be using the leash to extract him from under the nearest piece of furniture. Just let the cat lead, but also let him know that you and he are now connected by the leash.

After about a week of doing this for longer periods each day, add the following stage at what would normally be the end of your session. Step a few feet in front of the cat, kneel or lie at his level, hold out a morsel of his favourite treat, give your "come" command and very slightly tug on the leash – don't pull the cat. In another week you'll be ready to forget the morsel of food and reward the cat with praise alone. Increase the distance until you've persuaded the cat into something resembling an actual walk on the leash.

You and your cat are now more than a month from the beginning of this training period. Now you can attempt your first actual outing. The garden is the most non-threatening location for this and the next few trials. Finally, when the two of you are strolling about the yard, comfortable with each other's role in this strange affair, try walking in a nearby park.

CHAPTER THIRTEEN

Trespassers
will be shot on sight

ew of the neighbourhood cats even tried to challenge Tiger on his "turf" any longer. For that matter, few creatures of any sort in the neighbourhood were foolhardy enough to encroach on the acre or so of ground, trees, garden, driveway, garage and house that he claimed as his territory.

The dog and human family with whom Tiger shared his home were permitted to roam freely throughout the site, but even they tended to respect the scarred feline scrapper and give him quarter more often than not.

So Tiger lived for the occasional wandering stray from outside the neighbourhood. He relished every such opportunity to add to his legend, which over the years included wins beyond those of even the most able prize-fighters. Other male cats accounted for the majority of his "notches", but many a day – and an occasional raccoon or opossum – retreated before his ferocity. Without knowing it, we often reinforced Tiger's dominance over the site by breaking up a fight and chasing the intruding cat.

At about the age of five, in the prime of his fighting career, Tiger met a challenger he just couldn't defeat. Like so many cats given free rein to roam unattended, Tiger ended his life beneath the wheels of some passing vehicle on the street in front of the tiny kingdom he had ruled over for so long.

We were never certain of what exactly had drawn him out into traffic. He had been content

LEFT *Nearly all cats like to keep an eye on other cats in the neighbourhood to ensure that the accepted territorial rules are being observed.*

LEFT *For the cat who is allowed outdoors, regular patrols of the territory are quickly turned into ritual behaviour that must be followed on every outing.*

CAT WATCHING TIP

You may not think your cat has a territory, but all cats do in some form. Follow your cat out into the garden. Make note of where it goes, what it looks at, what it marks, and how it reacts to other creatures in its proximity. Notice where it settles down and what paths it takes to get to where it wants to be. Note if there is also a common ground where it meets up with other cats, and what kind of social standing your cat seems to have as a member of the group. Do this for several days because the cat might not cover all its territory in just one.

to remain more or less within his territory prior to that fatal exception. Our buildings, fences, hedgerows and such had always seemed to suit him just fine for the boundaries of his domain.

Perhaps he had caught the scent of some female elsewhere in the neighbourhood or had found something objectionable about the food we had offered him that day. Except for those individual cats who are best described as having the wanderlust in their blood, mating and food are about the only things that will draw a cat from well-established territory.

Cats are perfectly happy to accept our man-made structures and contrivances as the boundaries to their territories, but not because they are

War Games

Cats may fight over territory, or a mate, but actual combat is always a last resort. More often, a ritual display of aggression is enough to see off an opponent. The combatants first investigate each other by sniffing at scent glands on the face (1). Swishing his tail, the aggressor sniffs the base of the opponent's tail and gives a threatening growl, putting the second cat on the defensive. The aggressor is now poised to strike (2) and the defensive cat crouches low, with ears and tail flat. The confrontation may end here, with the loser adopting a defensive posture and backing off (3). In this case the aggressor walks off disdainfully, leaving the loser to slink away. However, if the aggressor's challenge is met, fighting will ensue. The defendant first adopts the defensive threat, turning its body sideways and arching its back to look more imposing. The tail bristles and curls up (4). The aggressor, unimpressed, keeps on coming (5). The defendant crouches low, presses its ears flat to its head and hisses at its opponent. The pussyfooting is over (6). The aggressor pounces and the second cat defends itself by kicking out with its legs, claws out. The battle continues until the loser spots a chance to escape with as much dignity as it can muster.

following any direction on our part. No territory can be adequate, in the cat's opinion, unless it provides safe and secure places to sleep, eat and drink, relieve oneself, and play. And, in general, each of these places should be somewhat removed from all of the others. Even the cat that never gets beyond the confines of the house wants things this way. A litter box placed too close to the food bowl, therefore, may be the answer to a suddenly finicky cat.

ESTABLISHING TERRITORY

Territory size varies from one cat to the next and from one terrain to another. A cat in a small city apartment may claim only a couple of dozen square feet. A feral cat, living off the rodents and food scraps it can find in the streets, alleys and

ABOVE *An intruder brazenly breaks the territorial barrier, encroaching on the realm of a fellow feline who isn't able to fend off the assault just now.*

RIGHT *Territorial behaviour can be displayed toward non-cat species as well. Dogs are a particular target, but even humans can be told in no uncertain terms that they are trespassing.*

vacant buildings, may nightly roam many city blocks. A cat living on a farm in an isolated rural setting may lord over many, many acres.

Where the territories of two cats meet, there will generally be a small buffer zone of shared ground. We humans won't recognize this zone, but the cats have mutually agreed that they both may use this area for moving from one section of

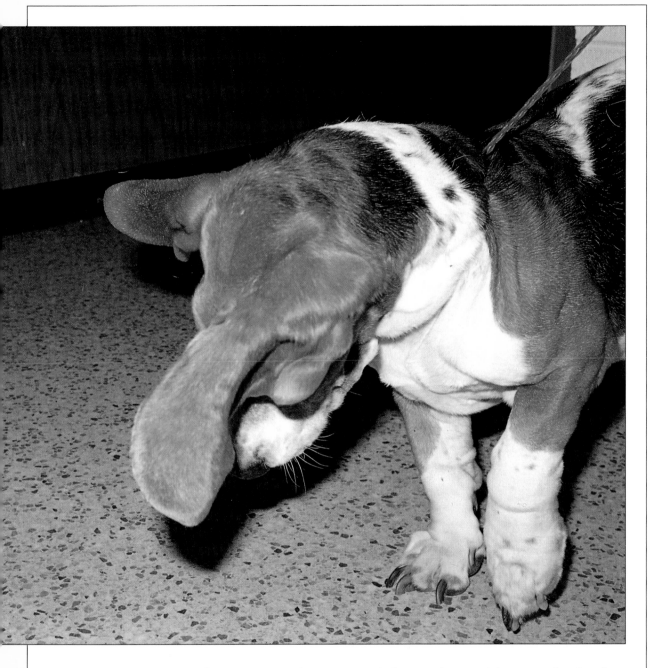

territory to the next or for hunting (only at different times).

A section of common ground is best described as the town hall. On this spot, which is claimed by no individual, the felines gather occasionally. Mating is often not the reason for their gatherings, as you might expect at first. Exactly what is "discussed" and "decided" has not yet been revealed to any human. These occasional gatherings do not negate our comments elsewhere in the book that cats are a good deal less social than many other creatures.

Ancestral instinct accounts for all this territorial behaviour. It comes down to our domestic cats from their forbears, who lived in the wild and fought every day for their continued existence.

ABOVE *Each cat usually has some elevated observation spot from which to oversee its territory. A relaxed posture when in this location should not be taken as letting down guard.*

LEFT *Territory size varies widely, depending upon the number of cats in a given area and the overall size of the area. A country cat may control acre after acre, while a city cat may be satisfied with a backyard or a balcony.*

Territorial Rules

The extent of a cat's territory depends on its position in the hierarchy. Queens with kittens (far right) have small territories which they defend fiercely. A tom (left) will probably have the most extensive area. All cats will avoid gardens where there is a dog, but some areas, such as paths, will be communal.

To those animals, the scent of food or their own waste too close to their sleeping area would certainly reveal their location to predators. In addition, the scents they left about their territory – both in their wastes and in glandular secretions – would warn off potential intruders of their own kind, who would otherwise compete with them for the essentials of life.

In the descendants of these wild ancestors the instinct still remains to claw the furniture like unleashed demons. How else will any intruding cats that happen along know that they are trespassing on someone else's territory?

Although nearly every cat needs some time to himself at regular intervals, those that share a house or garden with other cats may come to see that area as a jointly owned territory. In something akin to the much stronger pack behaviour in dogs, these cats will join together in the defence of their territory against all intruders.

An adaptation on this shared-territory scenario is a shift-work scheme in which the different cats actually take responsibility for guarding their grounds at different times. The other members of this "pack" will be found resting, eating, drinking or playing.

CHAPTER FOURTEEN

Why is my cat a lunatic?

If we've got across anything through this book, we hope it is this: cats are not little humans. They are animals that we share our homes and lives with, who have their own specific cat-needs and cat-desires.

With this concept firmly in mind, you'll be able to see all the "crazy" and "weird" things that your cats do as not really all that crazy or weird after all. Instead, you'll be able to understand and even appreciate them for the natural acts they really are.

One of the strangest of these is the catnip response, which has been described as everything from a health hazard that must be avoided at all costs to a lewd performance that should not be tolerated. Actually, it's nothing more than a simple, short-term and highly pleasurable intoxication. Through a chemical reaction with the aroma of catnip leaves, the cat's mind enters a state very similar to that which your own mind experiences after a few alcoholic beverages.

And, just like many a human, after having a taste the cat wants some more. Reverting to a near-kitten state, the cat rubs against the catnip, paws at it, tosses and catches it, eats it and smells it. However, unlike human intoxication, the

LEFT *Those cats who exhibit the catnip reaction should be allowed access to the plant or toys filled with its leaves for only limited periods to avoid building immunity to its effects.*

LEFT *Some plants can be toxic to cats that chew on their leaves. These should not be kept in a home shared with a cat.*

effect lasts only 15 to 30 minutes at a time. And, unlike human susceptibility to alcohol, cats can become physiologically immune to catnip if they smell it often.

This natural intoxication should not be regarded as a bad thing. Temporary and short-term, it is a great release for the animal. Cats are not the only non-human species to take advantage of the outlet intoxication can bring.

RIGHT *Many plants hold a special attraction for cats. This can be annoying to those people who try to maintain both felines and houseplants.*

It is not well known that the leaves of various plant species are sold under the common name of catnip. Nearly all of them, except genuine catnip (*Nepeta cataria*) hold nothing special for the cat. This true catnip has grey-green leaves and small, white, purple-spotted flowers.

There are a number of plants that hold a special fascination for cats – many dead and mutilated house-plants bear mute testimony to that fact.

However, there are a few that have qualities similar to those of catnip. They include boxwood, chickweed, cranberry, parsley, sage, silver vine, thyme, trumpet vine and valerian.

In addition, particular cats may nibble or claw at many other species of plants. Usually the cat has a fondness for the taste, smell or feel of the species that it singles out, but some cats just like attacking plants.

ABOVE *Scratching is a natural behaviour that cats must engage in to remove the sheaths of their old claws and allow for new growth. Declawing is a mutilating amputation and should not be considered as a solution to this problem.*

Some houseplants that you may want to avoid if you live with a nibbler include azalea, caladium, dieffenbachia, hedera ivy, laurel, mistletoe, oleander, philodendron, poinsettia and winter cherry. These all contain chemicals that are toxic to your cat.

A solution to persistent feline "gardeners" that some cat owners have found successful is to give the cat her own indoor garden box, planted with

OPPOSITE *To maintain their scentmarks around their territories, cats need to be let out for short periods quite often.*

various weeds, grasses and plants on the near–catnip list above. This is particularly true of cats who never go outdoors. You can soon teach her that these plants are intended for her enjoyment, but the rest of the plants in the house are strictly off–limits.

Scratching is another activity that many cat owners seek to eliminate in their pets. Cats do this, often with great enthusiasm and satisfaction, for the purpose of removing the old, outer sheaths from the claws of their front paws and allowing growth of the new claws beneath.

But, you say, they are satisfied with simply chewing the old sheaths from the claws of their rear paws. That's true, but the scratching action with the front paws also provides exercise for

ABOVE *As much as we work to understand our cats' emotions, thoughts and behaviours, they're always going to come up something new to treat us too . . . at least, let's hope so.*

Declawing

Under general anaesthetic, the claw is removed, along with the germinal cells responsible for its growth, and part or all of the terminal bone of the toe. This process leaves the animal without its principal means of defence.

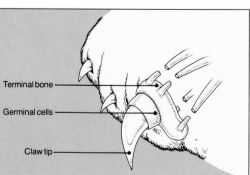

Terminal bone

Germinal cells

Claw tip

natural cat behaviour. And what reason can you really have for not providing a sturdy scratching post in some out-of-the-way place in the home?

Another "crazy" activity you might encounter with your cat is the out-in syndrome. In this annoying little pastime, Kitty first asks to be let out and then, almost immediately, asks to be let back in. Fifteen minutes later, she's ready for a repeat performance.

This process becomes easier to live with once you understand that Kitty needs only a very brief time to patrol her territory and check on the activity of neighbouring cats. However, she needs to make these patrols frequently to maintain the freshness and strength of the scentmarks that mark her territory, which also helps to maintain her comfort and security levels.

The out-in response is just one of the many instances when we poor, civilized humans sometimes simply haven't a clue as to what our cats

muscles running from the paws themselves all the way into the middle back. The scratching process also gives the feline one more mechanism for marking its territory. And finally, I don't think any of us can honestly say we haven't recognized the sheer joy that our cats get from a thorough scratching session.

As you can see, demanding that your cat cease scratching the furniture without providing an alternative is one more instance of trying to stifle

Declawing

The declawing of cats is never done in Britain except in cases of injury or disease but is widely practised in the United States. While this is not a book on cat health, the declawing issue warrants some mention in everything written about our feline friends. And the mention is this: don't do it.

Drop any illusions you might have about this. Declawing is amputation. It is not the simple clipping of a toenail – it is the full surgical removal of the last joint from each of the cat's toes.

Declawing is mutilation. With the claws goes the cat's primary means of defence, a considerable portion of his self-image and, as we've just discussed, a source of great pleasure. It is no wonder that declawed cats show a much increased tendency to biting and shyness.

are trying to tell us. Most of us have been away from the natural order of things for so many generations that we simply lack understanding at so basic a level. We dream of bigger cars, better vacations and the like, without ever giving much real thought to the basic needs that are the focus and driving force for the rest of life on earth. Our cats, as domesticated and tame as they may seem, still live that more basic life.

We and our cats face a communications barrier that can at times dwarf even the most complicated

ABOVE *Remember that psychological health and happiness for your cat relies on his being respected and* *treated as an animal with an animal's needs and desires – not as a furry little human.*

human-to-human language barrier. The human-to-cat barrier is a barrier of perspective. When we begin to look at things that relate to our cat from her perspective, we truly begin to move to the desired state where each one of us can say:

"I'm OK, my cat's OK."

Index

Page numbers in *italics* refer to picture captions.

Picture Credits

T = top; B = bottom; L = left; R = right

Norvia Behling: pp18, 20B, 102, 103, 111, 120, 124, 140. Bruce Berg: p14. C. B. Biedel: p36. Ed Birch: p59. Jeremy Bisley/Unicorn Stock Photographs: p90. Myer S. Bornstein: pp60, 64B. Arthur J. Boufford/Visuals Unlimited: p47. Kimberly Burnham/Unicorn Stock Photographs: p86B. Diane Calkins/Click the Photo Connection: pp2, 22, 39, 42, 63, 67, 85B, 112, 113, 134–5. Cleo Freelance Photography: pp23B, 108, 133. Tom Corner: p54T. W. Cortesi: pp8, 54B, 58, 122, 123. A. Corton/Visuals Unlimited: p75. A. J. Cunningham/Visuals Unlimited: pp26, 86T, 89, 136. John D. Cunningham/Visuals Unlimited: pp23T, 27, 72. Gail Denham: p17. Joel Dexter: pp49, 68. Jay Foreman: p77. Gerard Fritz/Photri Inc.: p94. Michael and Elvan Habicht: p81T. Chuck Hann: pp21, 43, 45, 71, 78T, 81B, 116T. Scott William Hanrahan: p12. Jim Hays: p61T. Arthur R. Hill: pp9L, 92. Linda Hopson/Visuals Unlimited: pp24, 44. C. Howe/Photri Inc.: p79. Kernel/Photri Inc.: p10B. K. King/Photri Inc.: p95. Erica Klass: p33T. Richard B. Levine: p37B. Tamara Liller Photography: pp66, 73B. Tom McCarthy: p76. Joe McDonald/Visuals Unlimited: p61B. Robert Marien: pp10T, 62, 93T. Dick Mermon: p134. Marie Mills and David Cummings/Unicorn Stock Photographs: p130B. D. Newman/Visuals Unlimited: pp34, 50, 69, 119B, 137. Duane Patten: pp97, 107, 117, 142. Paul A. Pavlik: pp52, 73T, 87. Permenter and Bigley: p11. Photri Inc.: pp25, 100, 119T. Jim Riddle/Unicorn Stock Photographs: p84. Frances Roberts: p31. Mae Scanlan: pp35, 37T, 38, 51, 93B, 101, 104, 106, 116, 128, 129L. Mrs Kevin Scheibel: pp29, 116B. Chuck Schmeiser: 132. Gregory K. Scott: pp32B, 33B, 47, 70, 80, 83, 96. Rosemary Shelton/Click the Photo Connection: pp13, 85T, 125, 143. John Sohlden/Visuals Unlimited: p57, 144. Larry Stanley: p15. C. Strock: pp7, 20T, 32T, 48, 55T, 99, 109. Emily Strong/Visuals Unlimited: p130T. Dave Underwood/Click the Photo Connection: pp53, 118. Garry Walter: p16. Sally Weigand: pp30, 41, 56, 64T, 65, 98, 105, 115. Richard West/Unicorn Stock Photographs: p88. Gerald L. Wicklund: pp6, 110.